TRACING YOUR HIST

ANCESTORS
THROUGH THE
EQUITY COURTS

D1612489

FAMILY HISTORY FROM PEN & SWORD

TRACING YOUR ANCESTORS THROUGH THE EQUITY COURTS

A Guide for Family and Local Historians

Susan T. Moore

Pen & Sword
FAMILY HISTORY

First published in Great Britain in 2017
PEN & SWORD FAMILY HISTORY
an imprint of
Pen & Sword Books Ltd
47 Church Street
Barnsley
South Yorkshire
S70 2AS

ISBN 978 1 47389 166 1

A CIP catalogue record for this book is
available from the British Library.

Typeset in Palatino and Optima by CHIC GRAPHICS

Printed and bound in England by
CPI Group (UK), Croydon, CR0 4YY

Pen & Sword Books Ltd incorporates the imprints of Pen & Sword
Archaeology, Atlas, Aviation, Battleground, Discovery, Family History,
History, Maritime, Military, Naval, Politics, Railways, Select, Social History,
Transport, True Crime, Claymore Press, Frontline Books, Leo Cooper,
Praetorian Press, Remember When, Seaforth Publishing and Wharncliffe.

For a complete list of Pen & Sword titles please contact
PEN & SWORD BOOKS LTD
47 Church Street, Barnsley, South Yorkshire, S70 2AS, England
E-mail: enquiries@pen-and-sword.co.uk
Website: www.pen-and-sword.co.uk

CONTENTS

Contents

LIST OF ILLUSTRATIONS

PREFACE

The records of the courts of equity are one of the most useful, if not *the* most useful of all sources for family history. I was first introduced to the records of the Court of Chancery many years ago when I was working as an apprentice genealogist. I was asked to make abstracts of a large number of cases relating to one family in a village in Hampshire. There were feuds and counter feuds, and that particular family's records kept me busy and very entertained for a life-changing week. That was my first introduction to Chancery records and their value to my historical research has in no way since diminished.

Since those early days I have regularly searched these enlightening records, studying not just the pleadings like those that first enthralled me, but also the myriad of related records, all of which can unearth fascinating information. It has become clear that these records can prove invaluable, not just for family historians but also for local and social historians.

Would your ancestor sit down to dinner with his brother? Would a butcher greet a fellow tradesman in the street? The records of the equity courts tell you who were friends and who were enemies. If people interest you, then the records of the courts of equity will keep you amused, interested, informed and enthralled in ways surpassing all other records.

Although the Court of Chancery was the most important of the courts of equity, there were others, and this book aims to introduce historians to the records of all these courts. The principles and processes, and thus the type of documents that were created, were similar in all the courts of equity. In this book examples are principally taken from the Court of Chancery, however they could have been chosen from any of the other courts of equity.

Although my first love is the Court of Chancery, the Court of the Star Chamber comes a close second. In a case from the reign of Henry VIII we are told of the attack made by Robert Cappis on his stepmother, 'a person of most ragyous and wilfull condicion' accompanied by three armed men, one of whom came 'with a vizer by cause he would not be known'. Robert suddenly plucked out his sword and threatened to run his stepmother through: 'thou step-dame by God's blood I care not though I thrust my sword through thee!' but was restrained by one of his companions. The stepmother it is said was in such dread and agony of mind that she fell ill, and as long as she lived would be the worse for his 'ragious' demeanour.[1]

In seeking examples for this book there is perhaps a preponderance of those from the West Country. This is simply because this is where I come from and what interests me most, and it does not denote any emphasis within the courts for this or any other geographical area. Examples could just as well have been taken from any part of the country.

The records of the courts of equity are all held at The National Archives (TNA) at Kew in London and although some can be identified online and copies provided from a distance, for most of the records it is necessary to travel in person to TNA or to employ the services of a specialist researcher such as myself who can undertake the research on your behalf.

My profound thanks must be offered to those who have helped with this book, in particular my postgraduates Alice Maltin, Helen Fanthorpe and Aurora Moxon who spent much of their summer transcribing and analysing records for use as examples, and all became experts on Chancery, despite now moving on to follow their own careers. Also to those who have read the text for me and offered much useful advice; I have received encouragement from many members of the staff at TNA, particularly Amanda Bevan and Liz Hore who very kindly read the text and in addition to making valuable suggestions, updated me with the online cataloguing programme. I am greatly indebted to John Wintrip for professionally indexing the book. Finally, my grateful thanks to all the friendly counter staff in the Map Room at TNA without whom none of us would be able to see any of the documents.

Susan Moore
July 2017

Chapter 1

BACKGROUND

Equity court records are one of the few that enable you to feel that you are getting to know the people involved, what sort of people they were, how they lived, what sort of disputes there were within their families and which members of the family might sit down at the dinner table together happily. But the records are not just about families, they shine a welcome light on the day-to-day life of people and businesses.

If you like reading about good people, and more particularly about bad people, people who may be telling the truth, and more certainly those who tell lies, then the courts of equity will provide some fascinating entertainment as well as useful historical information.

The records of the equity courts are of interest to family historians, house historians, local historians, social historians, business historians and legal historians.

WHAT ARE THE COURTS OF EQUITY?
Towards the end of the medieval period many citizens had grievances against other citizens which they wished to bring to the attention of the king, as they felt that the existing courts did not meet their needs. From this grew the courts of equity. The traditional courts, the Court of the King's Bench and the Court of Common Pleas, which dealt in common law had very proscriptive processes, and grievances often did not fit these, and moreover some felt that if their grievance was against a powerful man they did not have much chance of their case being heard fairly.

Henry Brougham, 1778–1868, Lord Chancellor.

According to J.H. Baker, despite power placed in the other courts, the king retained an overriding residuary power 'to do equal and right justice and discretion in mercy and truth'.[1] The king received so many Petitions for extraordinary relief that he could not deal with them in person. By the end of the fourteenth century officers to deal with these were the Chancellor, the Admiral and the Marshal. The most important was the Chancellor.

Equity or Law?
The courts of common law were courts of 'law' whereas the Court of Chancery was a court of 'equity'. It has been said that the law was 'no respecter of persons, and gave no relief to the foolish who fell

foul of its rigid rule'.[2] Equity acted 'in personam', that is it looked to the conscience of the individual. If that individual were obliged in conscience to do something such as perform a contract or restore property, the court of equity would order him to do it on pain of committal for contempt. Likewise, if he were bound in conscience to refrain from doing something he could be ordered to desist.

The principal difference between the common law courts and the equity courts was that the equity courts were based on what is right morally, whereas the common law courts relied on the law. The view of equity of Thomas Egerton, Master of the Rolls 1594–1603, was to 'correct mens' consciences for frauds, breaches of trust, wrongs and oppressions of what nature soever they be and to soften and mollify the extremity of the law'.[3]

From a researcher's point of view the principal difference is that the records of the courts of equity are written in English and are relatively easy to find, whereas the records of the common law courts are in Latin until 1733 and are not yet easy to navigate.

A real bonus is that the records are all held at TNA rather than being divided amongst a host of local record repositories.

There were a number of courts of equity:

- Chancery.
- Star Chamber.
- Requests.
- Exchequer.
- Duchy Chamber for Duchy of Lancaster.
- Palatinate of Durham.
- Exchequer of Chester.
- Welsh courts of equity.

The Court of Chancery

The Court of Chancery was the principal court of equity. Many of the examples of cases used in this book will be from the Court of Chancery, although they could equally well be taken from the other courts. Its origins are in the reign of Richard II (1377–99), and it continued to operate until 1876 when the courts were reorganised. Until that date the records are held under TNA reference C.

The Chancery was not a law court originally but was rather an administrative department with secretaries for the writing of treaties, grants and other public business over whom the Chancellor presided, and had no connection with any court of justice. It is thought that the word Chancery (*cancellaria* in Latin) originated with the latticed screen or chancel behind which the Chancery clerks worked. The Chancellor had custody of The Great Seal and much of the effort of the Chancery was administrative work such as authenticating royal grants. Until the reign of Henry VIII the Chancellors were Church men and 'served at the altar in spiritual things'.[4] Because of its Church origins the Court of Chancery dealt with 'conscience' rather than 'law'. It was said to gain its authority from the king who was God's representative. This type of court, based on conscience, was known as a court of equity rather than a court of common law.

There was considerable rivalry between the common law courts and the Court of Chancery as the lawyers who worked in the common law courts felt that the Chancery clerks did not have any legal training and so were unfit to dispense justice. By the mid-sixteenth century there was a move to change this and Sir Thomas More (1478–1535) was the first Chancellor with a legal background.

Advantages of the Court of Chancery

There were four categories of case where the Court of Chancery would be preferred over one of the common law courts.

1. Not under the jurisdiction of common law:

- The case concerned a mortgage or a trust.
- Cases where specific information, usually held by the other side, is required to make a case. This might be in the form of supplying a copy of grant of land, or accounts or copy of a will.

John Scott, Lord High Chancellor of England, 1801–6, by William Cowen.

- An injunction could be sought by the plaintiff to prevent the defendant from carrying out an action such as cutting down valuable trees on a property which the plaintiff believed should be his.
- The plaintiff was not in possession of the relevant documents to establish his title to lands or property.
- If a creditor died before a debt was repaid, the executors of the deceased creditor could not be sued under common law, but the plaintiff could bring a case against the creditor in the Court of Chancery.

- An agreement had been made verbally with no supporting documents.

2. The case could be heard under common law but it was felt that no remedy could be obtained:

- Plaintiff might be too poor to afford common law courts.
- Plaintiff might be a weak person compared with the defendant, such as when a tenant was bringing a case against a mighty landlord.

3. The common law was being used oppressively or fraudulently:

- Plaintiff feared local corruption or a prejudiced jury.
- Plaintiff was afraid of being harmed by the defendant.

4. Case brought on the grounds of forgery or duress:

- Plaintiff could not recover money which the defendant had improperly deprived him of under the common law.
- Where the plaintiff was owed money by the defendant, but the defendant might have obtained a release or receipt from the plaintiff by fraud.

One of the principal differences in the jurisdiction of the common law courts and the Court of Chancery was that the Court of Chancery was concerned with the possession or occupation of land whereas the common law courts were concerned with the legal ownership of land, whereas generally the possession of the land, rather than the ultimate legal owner was what concerned people, as so much land was held in trust or mortgaged.

Star Chamber
This court dealt principally with equity cases where violence was involved and these records make for lively reading. The court had a

much shorter lifespan than the Court of Chancery, also coming into being in the late medieval period but abolished in 1641. The court has an emotional appeal to many researchers such as: 'Lambarde's rosy view of the Star Chamber "this most noble and praiseworthy court the beams of whose bright justice, equal in beauty with Hesperus and Lucifer . . . do blaze and spread themselves as far as the realm is long and wide"'.[5]

The origin of the name 'Star Chamber' has many theories. Many believe that it derives from the stars that adorned the ceiling of the room in which it met. Others believe that it comes from the Anglo-Saxon 'steoran' meaning to steer or govern. There are those who think that it came from the fact that the room where the court sat was the depository of the Jewish bonds called 'Starra', others again think that it derives from the judges who, like stars, shone in the legal world deriving light from the royal sun!

The starred chamber was known in the reign of Edward III as a place where the king's Council met to do justice on great offenders who were too powerful for the ordinary courts to deal with effectively. Although the court was active intermittently until the start of the reign of Henry VII, the effective starting date for the court was an Act of Parliament in 1487 and a further Act in the reign of Elizabeth I.[6]

The Act of 1487 first rehearsed the particular mischiefs it was designed to check such as maintenance, the giving of liveries, signs and tokens, retainers by indenture, promises, oaths, writing or otherwise, embraciaries of the king's subjects, the untrue demeaning of Sheriffs in making panels and other untrue returns, corruption of juries, great riots and unlawful assemblies. It then gave the Chancellor, Treasurer and Keeper of the Privy Seal authority to summon before them, by writ of privy seal, the misdoers, examine them at their discretion and punish them according to law.

Thus armed, this powerful court became a terror to the evil doers whose violence brought them within its sphere. Riot, bullying of all kinds, tyranny, oppression and contempt for the weak found prompt, swift justice, free from red tape and formalism.

In comparison with the ordinary law courts the Star Chamber was both swift and cheap and its rapid action did much to secure its hold on the people.

Records survive from about 1476 to 1641 under TNA reference STAC.

Court of Requests

This court was known as the poor man's court, and dealt with equity cases of low value. Like the Court of the Star Chamber, it has origins in the very late medieval period and was abolished in 1641. The Court of Requests, also like the Court of the Star Chamber, had its origins in the Privy Council, although it was never placed on a statutory basis.

This court concentrated on 'the expedition of poore mennys causes' and was originally called the Court of Poor Men's Causes, rather than the Court of Requests which name was first used in 1529. Although there was originally no rule to say that litigants had to be poor, it was used principally by those who were less well off and whose cases were of insufficient value to qualify for the Court of Chancery. In 1588 and then again in 1618, ordinances were passed expressly referring poor plaintiffs to this court.

Like the other courts, it was itinerant originally, following the king's progress around the country, but Cardinal Wolsey oversaw its establishment in the White Hall at Westminster from 1517. It was however still seen as one of the committees of the Privy Council, rather than a proper court of law. By the end of the reign of Henry VIII it was composed of professional lawyers with the judges being called Masters of Requests.

Records survive from about 1485 to 1641 under TNA reference REQ.

Court of the Exchequer

Originally this court dealt with equity cases which involved payments to the Crown, but later it became an alternative to the Court of Chancery. It dealt with all cases, and was sometimes

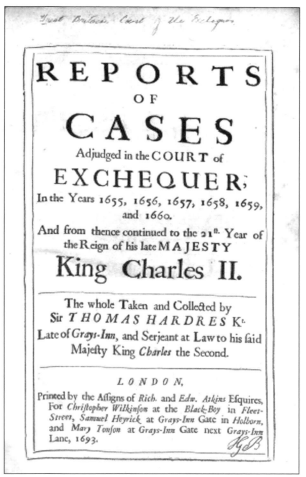

Reports of cases in the Court of Exchequer.

preferred as its processes were thought to be quicker than those of the Court of Chancery. Over 100,000 cases were heard in this court. Until the mid-seventeenth century litigants had to have some genuine connection with the royal revenue, as officials or tenants of the Crown. From 1649 onwards it became rather more open to anyone. In 1841 the court was merged with the Court of Chancery.

It has been said that the equity side of the Court of the Exchequer is 'by far the most obscure of all the English jurisdictions'.[7] This court, however, is of importance to researchers as so many cases were heard during the two centuries of its greatest activity – the seventeenth and eighteenth centuries. The origins of this court are lost in the mists of time, but its separate use as an equity court dated probably no further back than the mid-sixteenth century. At this time the exchequer was divided into two: the 'upper exchequer' or 'exchequer of account' and the 'lower exchequer' or 'exchequer of receipt'. The lower exchequer handled the cash and the upper exchequer handled the accounting of the royal revenues. It is from this latter that the equity court developed. There were three distinct offices, each with their own personnel, and each of which developed legal jurisdiction:

- The king's remembrancer's office – cases between monarch and private person.
- The lord treasurer's remembrancer's office – cases between monarch and private person.
- The office of pleas – cases between private parties.

It is the office of pleas that developed into the equity court and was truly established by the mid-sixteenth century and peaked in the late seventeenth century. Despite its popularity as a court, it never handled as many cases as the Court of Chancery.

Originally the people who could use the Court of the Exchequer were:

- Officers of the exchequer.
- Servants of the officers.
- Debtors to the Crown.

In order to qualify as a debtor to the Crown a fiction had developed by 1649 whereby one person could sue another over any sort of matter if it could be argued that it affected the plaintiff's ability to pay any debts that he might have which were due to be paid to the Crown. From this date we see the Court of the Exchequer being regarded as a general court of equity rather than one specialising in royal revenue. This was probably connected to the fact that the Court of the Star Chamber was abolished in 1641, the Court of Requests ceased to operate from this date, and the equity jurisdictions of the council in the north and the council in the Marches of Wales also fell into abeyance.

Records are available from 1558 to 1841 under TNA reference E.

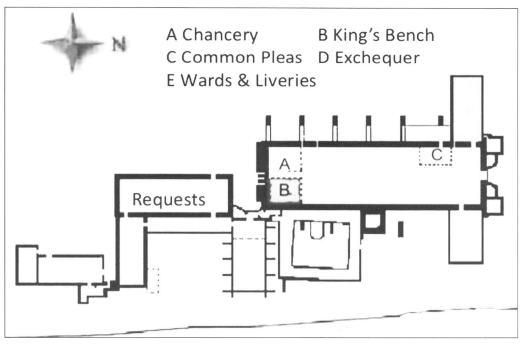

A Chancery   B King's Bench
C Common Pleas   D Exchequer
E Wards & Liveries

The layout of the courts of equity in Westminster Hall.

Duchy of Lancaster

The equity court of the Duchy of Lancaster, known as the Court of Duchy Chamber, had jurisdiction over the lands that made up the Duchy, which are not restricted to the county of Lancashire, but includes areas over almost the whole country. In 1351 Edward III created the first Duke of Lancaster. When Henry IV, as successor to the first Duke of Lancaster, became king in 1399, his Lancaster inheritance did not merge with the other Crown estates, but remained separate, and included all his estate not just the lands within the county of Lancashire. The court of equity was based in London. The principal officer was the Chancellor of the Duchy of Lancaster.

The records of the Duchy of Lancaster court of equity survive from 1474 to 1872 under TNA reference DL.

The Palatinates

A palatinate was an area over which a bishop or duke possessed royal privileges and had jurisdiction which elsewhere belonged to the sovereign alone. These rights included a court of equity.

PALATINATE OF LANCASTER

The county of Lancaster initially became a palatinate when in 1351 Edward III conferred the title of duke on Henry Earl of Lancaster and granted him palatine rights within the county of Lancashire. There was a certain merging of the Palatinate of Lancaster and the Duchy of Lancaster in 1399, but the two remain essentially separate.

The records of the Palatinate of Lancaster court of equity survive principally from 1612 to 1853, with a few records in the period 1490 to 1611 under TNA reference PL.

PALATINATE OF DURHAM

In medieval times the Bishop of Durham ran what almost amounted to a parallel kingdom with similar powers and rights over lands within the bishopric which was virtually the same as the county of Durham. The court was operating as a court of equity by the late fifteenth or early sixteenth centuries. The chief officer was the Chancellor who was usually a lawyer. Most records from before the seventeenth century have been lost. Apart from the usual subject matter of any court of equity a large number of cases in this court related to the revenues of the Bishops of Durham and to the enclosure of common lands.

Records for the Palatinate of Durham court of equity survive from 1576 to 1840 under TNA reference DURH.

PALATINATE OF CHESTER

As with the Palatinate of Lancaster, the Earl of Chester had power over the palatinate, which included the counties of Cheshire and Flint. The court of equity was known as the Exchequer of Chester. The chief officer of the court was the Vice Chamberlain who was usually a lawyer. Other officials included the Baron of the Exchequer, who was similar to a Master in Chancery.

The records of the Palatinate of Chester court of equity run from about 1509 to 1830, although the court declined in importance after 1660, under TNA reference CHES.

Wales

The jurisdiction of the Welsh equity courts are not as clear-cut as those of the Palatinates. There were equity courts for three circuits in Wales: North Wales circuit covering Anglesey, Carnarvon and Merioneth; Brecon Circuit covering Brecon, Radnor and Glamorgan; and the Carmarthen Circuit covering Carmarthen, Pembroke and Cardigan. Whereas the courts of equity of the Palatinate courts were more or less exclusive to their geographical area, this is certainly not true of the Welsh cases, and many are found in the more mainstream national courts.

Records for the Wales courts of equity survive from 1689 to 1830 and were classed originally under TNA reference WALES, however most of the records have been transferred to the National Library of Wales.

This book will cover the records of all these Courts of Equity, except the court for Wales as the records are not held at TNA, and will concentrate on their relevance to historians and researchers. This book is not a treatise on legal practice.

FURTHER READING

There are some excellent books that give very much more detail on the history and workings of the courts of equity, and these are listed in the Select Bibliography. Two that must be highlighted are the ones by Henry Horwitz and Louis Knafla, who have both studied particular periods of the courts. Henry Horwitz writes on the Court of Chancery 1600 to 1800 and the Court of the Exchequer from 1641 to 1841.[8] Louis Knafla writes about just one year, 1602, as it relates to Kent, but has a wealth of background material.[9]

DORMANT FUNDS AND MONEY IN CHANCERY
Many people believe that 'money held in Chancery' means that there will be a case in the Chancery court of equity. This is not so, and the records of the dormant funds are in the Court Funds Office, and the Unclaimed Balance Index is the best place to start a search.

WHO SHOULD LOOK AT THESE RECORDS?
As with so much to do with the records of the courts of equity, the question should perhaps be 'who should *not* look at these records'. Family historians will probably have the most benefit from looking at the records, as they can prove several generations in one go, and give a wonderful insight into the life and character of family members. However the records should not be ignored by:

- Local historians who will gain detailed information on a farm, town, industry, charitable organisation or common land that is not available in any other records.
- House historians who will find much personal information about former inhabitants of their house. On occasion reference to the building or rebuilding of a house will be included. If the house was let, then often the amount of the rent can be found along with the names of the tenants.
- Social historians who will be most interested in the many accounts and financial statements that survive within the records.
- Business historians who will learn about disputes between business colleagues, partners, customers, and means of trade and banks.

- Railway historians who will learn of disputes involving the early railway companies.

Those who will probably not gain any information are historians of the early medieval period before the advent of these courts, or those of the second half of the twentieth century. Having said this, many cases start with a history of their case, and this can go back many years well into the early medieval period. Even political historians can gain benefit from these records, particularly for more background information on Members of Parliament.

HELPFUL PRIOR KNOWLEDGE
In order to research the records of the courts of equity, certain skills are needed. These do not include an ability to read Latin as the records are in English.

Palaeography
An ability to read standard documents of the period is essential as until the mid-nineteenth century all records are handwritten. From the latter half of the nineteenth century some records are printed.

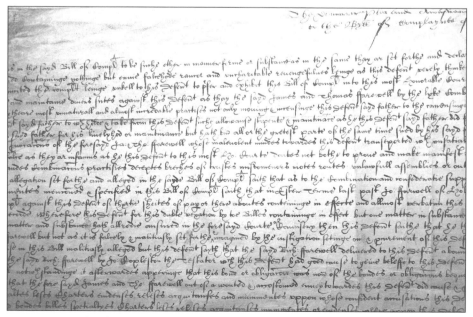

An example of palaeography from the Court of Star Chamber.

The records of the courts of equity consist of many different types of record. The principal records, the Bills and Answers or Pleadings, are written in much the same handwriting as the Prerogative Court of Canterbury registered wills. Other records, such as the depositions or witness statements, can be written in a much more hurried hand, and are therefore less easy to read. The handwriting in these often resembles handwritten wills as opposed to the writing found in registered copies. The handwriting in the Orders and Depositions is usually not difficult; the challenge with these records comes from understanding the many abbreviations. The other records within the courts of equity are generally not challenging for those who can read the Pleadings.

Understanding of Wills

A great number of cases in the courts of equity, particularly those in the Court of Chancery, concern disputes over wills. Many relate in some way to unclear wording, such as whether a bequest or annuity was to come from the real or personal estate of the testator, others concern bequests that have not been made by the executors. Familiarity with the terms used in wills, is therefore very useful in understanding the equity court records. Wills are often partially quoted, and on occasion can be quoted in full. The court of probate is often also mentioned, which can help in tracking down an elusive will.

Understanding of Deeds

Another common source of dispute in the courts of equity is the interpretation of mortgages, marriage settlements and deeds of entail. These deeds are often quoted in full in the court cases. Unlike today, in the past when a piece of land was given as security for a loan, even when there was a date for repayment, if repayment was not made the land did not automatically become transferred to the mortgagee. There exist cases where, several generations after the date of the mortgage, the heir of the original holder of the land claims that it should be his, arguing that the mortgagee has received

16

the rents from the land which amount to the repayment of the capital with interest. Marriage settlements can lead to all sorts of disputes, a favourite being where a second wife is claiming the same land that the eldest son by the first wife believes should be his. These sorts of disputes can be full of interesting and useful information for both family and local historians.

In view of this, a familiarity with different types of deed and the ability to interpret them will be very helpful in understanding this sort of equity case.

The Legal Terms

Many of the records are arranged by legal term. These are Hilary, Easter, Trinity and Michaelmas and records such as the Orders and Decrees are arranged, and calendared, by term.

The law terms varied to a certain extent because of the variable date of Easter, and they ran approximately:

Michaelmas term:	October to November
Hilary term:	January to February
Easter term:	April to May
Trinity term:	June to July

Some knowledge of the law terms is necessary as many of the contemporary indexes and calendars are arranged by law term. For the exact dates of terms in any year, see the tables in Cheney, such as:[10]

1600	Hilary	23 January to 12 February
	Easter	9 April to 5 May
	Trinity	23 May to 11 June
	Michaelmas	9 October to 28 November
1700	Hilary	23 January to 12 February
	Easter	17 April to 13 May
	Trinity	31 May to 19 June
	Michaelmas	23 October to 28 November

1800	Hilary	23 January to 12 February
	Easter	30 April to 26 May
	Trinity	13 June to 2 July
	Michaelmas	6 November to 28 November

Understanding of Legal Words

Most of the records of the courts of equity are written in normal, if slightly stylised, English and do not require any legal knowledge. Occasionally there are references to legal processes of the common law courts, such as when a case is brought to a court of equity in order to obtain an injunction to put a temporary stop on a common law court case and reference is made to the particular writ used in the common law case. When such words are encountered, definitions are easily found in legal dictionaries. Most equity records do not contain any such words.

The clerks of court learnt how to word Chancery cases in a reasonably standard way from such publications as *The Compleat Clerk* which included: 'the best forms of all sorts of presidents for conveyances and assurances, and other instruments now in use and practice: with the forms of bills, pleadings, and answers in chancery as they were penned and perfected by eminent lawyers'.[11]

Ability to Concentrate

The documents, particularly after the mid-seventeenth century tend to be very long winded and repetitive, so a good ability to concentrate is necessary. Generally it is worth making a full transcript of each document, with a section for a summary at the end, which can be written as the full transcript is being made and the different points at issue come to light. The documents are generally physically large. Those from the early nineteenth century can measure 3ft × 4ft and consist of as many as ten pages. The very early ones before 1558 are usually much smaller and more concise, and are therefore rather easier to work with.

OVERVIEW OF THE DOCUMENTS
Broad Description
The records of the courts of equity all follow a similar pattern, so understanding the process of one of the courts is a way into the records of all the other courts, even if the references and level of indexing varies from one court to another.

Each case can consist of many different types of record, and following a case through the court can be very rewarding in terms of giving an insight into individual people's lives, relationships with family member and social relationships with those around them.

The records of the equity courts are one of the few historical records that can recite the history and relationships of many generations, thus clarifying the existence of several people of the same name within a family, giving dates of marriage and death, and, in the case of the Court of the Star Chamber, adding a bit of spice to the research with the description of the violence that is claimed to have taken place for a case to qualify for being heard in this court.

Jurisdiction of the Courts
The main courts had jurisdiction over England and Wales. Scotland had a separate system. Having said this, there are cases that involve people and properties all over the world, including Scotland. There are a good number of cases brought by people in America even after 1776, although there are more cases before independence, and there are many cases involving those in India and the East India Company.

Bills and Answers and Depositions
These records form the backbone for research and are often referred to as the Pleadings. Each case in a court of equity starts with the plaintiff putting in a **Bill of Complaint** in which the case is set out. First the background is given and this can often be the most useful part for family historians, such as when a phrase starts with 'my great grandfather . . .', then the matter at issue is set out, and finally specific points are outlined that the defendant should answer.

The defendant then puts in an **Answer**, usually following the order of points made in the Bill of Complaint and either agreeing with or denying each point. Additional new information will often also be outlined, which can give a very different complexion to the case as it was made by the plaintiff.

The next stage is the taking of **Depositions** from witnesses. The plaintiff and the defendants each compile a list of questions (known as interrogatories) that they put to their chosen witnesses (known as deponents). The deponents then each answer the questions that are relevant to them. For those living within easy reach of London the Depositions were heard in London, for others a trip to the local inn was usually what was needed, as the person appointed by the lawyers would travel to the locality, install himself in the inn, and take down the answers from each of the deponents. These written answers to the Interrogatories are the Depositions that we have now.

In addition to the sometimes considerable light that Depositions can shine on the substance of the case, each Deposition starts with the name, abode, age and occupation of the deponent. Thus, some quite humble people can find their way into the records. The first question usually asks whether the deponent knows the plaintiff and defendant, and if so, for how long they have known them. This can elicit very useful genealogical information such as 'since birth' or 'for two years since I moved here from the parish of xx', thus helping to determine how long someone has been in a parish, and where they came from.

Decrees and Orders

In addition to the Bills and Answers, and the Interrogatories and Depositions, there are many other records that can be involved in a case in a court of equity. The Decrees and Orders are the simplest to locate and to use. For the Court of Chancery the handwritten calendars are on the open shelves in the reading room at TNA, and are arranged chronologically by law term, then alphabetically by the initial letter of the surname. The reference number in the calendar is to the folio number in the register of Decrees and Orders. Some of the Decrees and Orders are very dull, and concern the administrative process, such as ordering a defendant to submit his answer, but others can be very informative, and summarise the case, with the order. By the nineteenth century many Decrees and Orders concern applications for the distribution of money, and reference is given within the Orders to other useful documents, such as Affidavits and Petitions.

Affidavits

These are witness statements given voluntarily by people under oath who feel they have something to add to the case, but have not been called by the plaintiff or the defendant to give answers to Interrogatories. They could concern a defendant who is unable to appear, or to substantiate objections. Although the class of documents for the Court of Chancery dates from 1611, they do not really become useful sources of new information until the nineteenth century. From 1615 to1747 there is a register of Affidavits which runs parallel to the files of Affidavits.

Petitions

These are particularly useful source for the nineteenth century in the Court of Chancery and run from 1774 to 1875. Before 1834 they consist only of appeal Petitions against unenrolled Decrees and Orders, but after that date they also include many applications for payment, and the administration of estates.

Cause Books

These books act as a summary of the cases in the Court of Chancery, listing the dates of appearances and documents, with brief reference to Decrees and Orders, and particularly for the period 1842 to 1880, and are a very useful way of getting into a case, and seeing what documents exist other than the basic Bills and Answers.

Masters' Reports

Not all cases proceeded as far as needing a Master's Report, but where they do exist they are an invaluable summary of the case, based not just on the Bills and Answers, but on all the supplementary documents and also external evidence such as wills and deeds. On occasion they can be very lengthy and mostly concern the administration of estates following a dispute over a will. They can also concern lunatics and infant wards of court. They are usually requested in an Order, so that further information can be gathered, such as the financial statements of the parties. The report itself will often include detailed accounts.

Masters' Exhibits
This series consists of the documents that were used as evidence in the case. Generally these were returned to their owners once the case had drawn to a close, but on occasion they were never collected and remained with the Master. In some instances the documents remain, but the case to which they refer is no longer noted and they are listed simply as being from an Unknown Cause.

Masters' Documents
These documents are usually internal to the case, and consist of Depositions, Affidavits, accounts and other documents that were needed for the Master to compile his report. These records are not easy to access at present.

Masters' Accounts
These provide a useful overview of property in question for the later eighteenth and nineteenth centuries.

Who Brought Cases?
It is sometimes thought that only the wealthy brought cases to the court. This is emphatically not true. People who feature in the courts of equity come from all sorts of background including, but by no means limited to:

Aristocracy
Gentlemen
Merchants

Ship masters
Yeomen
Tradesmen – cordwainers, carpenters, bakers, fishmongers, etc.
Farmers
Manorial tenants
Labourers
Prisoners
Manufacturers and industrialists
Banks
Emigrants including those in America
Jews
Clergymen
Companies – industrial, East India Company, Hudson's Bay
   Company, etc.
Residents of India

Even more helpfully, the courts of equity are one of the few classes of document where women and children feature regularly. It is worth remembering that a child, or 'infant' the word usually used, is defined as a person under the age of 21. Women feature in the cases in their own right, before marriage, during marriage and after marriage, i.e. as widows, spinsters and wives.

There is scarcely a type of person who does not make an appearance in these records, although, as a rule of thumb, it is more usual for those who might have left a will to be of the social standing that would encourage them to initiate a dispute in a court of equity. More humble people certainly appear, but usually incidentally rather than bringing cases to court.

Where do the Parties Come From

The simple answer to this is: anywhere and everywhere. Obviously, most cases concern England and Wales, where the courts of equity had jurisdiction, however, cases can be found involving places as far afield as Virginia, Calcutta, Norway, Scotland and Africa to mention just a few.

THE BEST PERIODS TO SEARCH

There are two reasons why one might prefer to search one period or another for a case in a court of equity, particularly the Chancery or Exchequer courts: how well they are indexed or calendared, and how many cases there were at the period. Henry Horwitz in his books on the Chancery and Exchequer Courts analysed the number of new cases in sample years.[12]

Court of Chancery

Horwitz's figures show that the numbers of cases increased from the late medieval and early modern period to the late seventeenth century. There was a gradual decline in the number of new cases during the eighteenth century, but this was countermanded by an increase in the time each took, so that the number of active cases in 1818 was similar to the number of active cases in 1684.

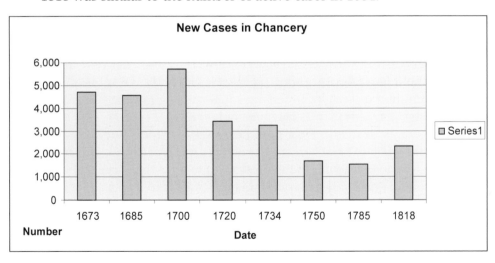

A study of the Court of Chancery as it relates to Kent in the period 1558 to 1602 shows that the number of new cases increased significantly after about 1585, with a peak of cases in 1597.[13] The decision by a researcher as to whether or not to search for a Chancery case will depend as much as anything on the completeness of the indexing and detailed online entries in TNA's catalogue. Periods where there is full indexing with the names of all the parties and place names given are likely to take precedence over those where only the surnames of the principal plaintiff and defendant are given. The fact that place names are not yet given in the online catalogue for all periods means that local historians will be more limited in their use of Chancery records, unless the names of the principal families of the locality are known.

Chancery After 1876

In 1876 there was an overhaul of the legal system. Chancery cases continued to be heard in the Supreme Court and the records are similar to those before 1876. The calendars are less helpful, but newspaper reports can often be the easiest way of finding a case.

The Court of the Exchequer

As with the Court of Chancery the number of new cases reduced from its heyday in the late seventeenth century, with 650 cases being brought in 1685 and just 374 by 1819 with a bit of a revival in the late eighteenth century when 450 new cases are shown as being brought to the court in 1785.[14]

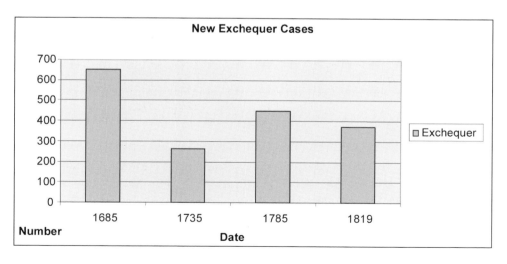

LAWYERS AND THE INNS OF CHANCERY

The lawyers who worked on Chancery cases were usually attached to one of the Inns of Chancery.

The Inns of Chancery, based in London, were predominantly a group of preparatory institutions for trainee lawyers aspiring to join the Inns of Court. The four Inns of Court (which remain today) were the formal professional associations where lawyers lived, trained and worked.

Although it is hard to date the Inns of Chancery (and indeed the Inns of Court) precisely, evidence shows that they were operational in the fourteenth century. The name originated from their first purpose – as a place for the Clerks of Chancery to lodge and prepare their writs. Students would come to observe them and learn their craft, and to gain a basic understanding of law before continuing their learning at the Inns of Court. In addition to their educatory function, the Inns of Chancery provided accommodation and offices for solicitors, who carried out correspondence duties there. It is interesting to note that it was not just intending lawyers who attended the Inns of Chancery and the Inns of Court. For many elite families these institutions were seen as an excellent way for young men to further their education and to make valuable connections with other influential members of society.

Most of the Inns of Chancery were attached to a particular Inn of Court (Inns of Court charged higher fees to students from independent Inns of Chancery), and they were built in clusters around them. Periodically, readers would be sent by the Inns of Court to give lectures and supervise the students. Training at the Inns of Chancery would take about two years before promising students were moved on to an Inn of Court.

This original system underwent many changes which led to the eventual dissolution of the Inns of Chancery. Perhaps the most significant change was after the first English Civil War. In 1642 the Inns of Court began to exclude attorneys and solicitors, and by the turn of the eighteenth century they were almost exclusively for barristers and trainee barristers. As a result, the Inns of Chancery became much more heavily dedicated to the needs of solicitors, boasting various associations and offices for them. Most trainee barristers now chose to apply directly to the Inns of Court, bypassing the Inns of Chancery altogether.

The consequent founding of the Society of Gentlemen Practisers in 1739 followed by The Law Society in 1825 provided solicitors with a unified professional association and rendered the Inns of Chancery virtually redundant. At first they remained as places for solicitors to dine and socialise, but by 1900 almost all the Inns of Chancery had been sold.

Individual Inns of Chancery

It is thought that many smaller Inns of Chancery may have existed of which there are no record; we have more information about those attached to the Inns of Court. The four Inns of Court are: Inner Temple, Middle Temple, Lincoln's Inn and Gray's Inn.

CLIFFORD'S INN, ATTACHED TO THE INNER TEMPLE

Clifford's is thought to be the oldest of the Inns of Chancery – there is evidence that part of the Inn was let out to law students as early as 1344. Most of the Inn was knocked down in 1934, although a gatehouse still remains. Two panes of glass from its hall were extracted and kept at the Inner Temple Library, only to be destroyed in the Blitz.

CLEMENT'S INN, ATTACHED TO THE INNER TEMPLE

Clement's Inn was located just to the west of the Royal Courts of Justice. William Shakespeare is amongst its alumni, as is his fictional character Justice Shallow from *Henry IV, Part II*:

> 'He must to the Inns of Court. I was of Clement's once myself, where they talk of Mad Shallow still.'
>
> *Henry IV, Part II*, Act iii, a

The members of Clement's sold the Inn in 1884 and the building was demolished in 1891.

LYON'S INN, ATTACHED TO THE INNER TEMPLE
Lyon's Inn was originally a hostel before being turned into an Inn of Chancery. Situated in current-day Aldwych, Lyon's was widely considered a disreputable institution when it was dissolved.

STRAND INN, ATTACHED TO THE MIDDLE TEMPLE
Also known as Chester Inn, Strand Inn was a short-lived endeavour. It was pulled down in the mid-sixteenth century to make way for Somerset House and its students were moved to New Inn.

NEW INN, ATTACHED TO THE MIDDLE TEMPLE
New Inn was originally called St George's Inn or Our Lady's Inn. Sir Thomas More was a student here. Its buildings were pulled down to make way for a road.

FURNIVAL'S INN, ATTACHED TO LINCOLN'S INN
Founded in about 1383, Furnival's Inn was once home to Charles Dickens. It was sold by Lincoln's Inn in 1888, and demolished about a decade later.

The site of Furnival's Inn.

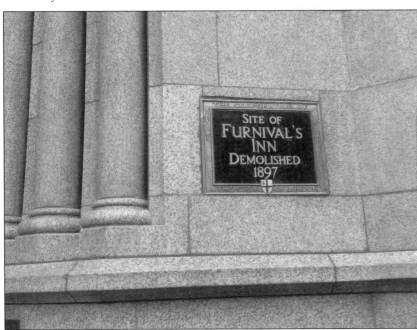

THAVIES INN, ATTACHED TO LINCOLN'S INN
Thavie's Inn dates back to the mid-fourteenth century and was sold in 1772.

STAPLE INN ATTACHED TO GRAY'S INN
Staple Inn is the only Chancery Inn still standing today, the original building dating from about 1415. The Inn's coat of arms includes a bale of wool; it was once a wool merchant's. Although Staple Inn was badly damaged by a bomb in 1944, it was skilfully restored and rebuilt. Formerly part of the headquarters of the Institute of Actuaries, since 2012 the building has been used to host several of their meetings and events.

BARNARD'S INN, ATTACHED TO GRAY'S INN
Barnard's Inn was originally known as Mackworth's Inn after John Mackworth, its owner. Barnard's implemented a curious practice of fining students for mistakes; for example, if you used a 'defective' word you were charged a halfpenny.

Barnard's Inn.

Chapter 2

WHY LOOK AT THE COURTS OF EQUITY?

This section of the book looks at the benefits of researching the records of the courts of equity. The type of information available is true of all the different courts, although most of the examples are taken from the Court of Chancery, being the busiest of the courts and also the one where the records are most easily accessible.

WHAT SORT OF INFORMATION MIGHT BE FOUND IN BILLS AND ANSWERS?

This heading should perhaps be rephrased 'what sort of information would not be found in Bills and Answers?'. The records are so full of information of all types, that there is little that cannot be found in a case somewhere. If a researcher wants to know about the family other than the bare names, dates and parishes, the records of the courts of equity are a must.

The Bills and Answers form the backbone of the equity courts, indeed many cases never proceed beyond this stage. A parish register will usually only locate a family within a parish, a will might give a little more information, but a case brought to an equity court can describe in much more detail where a family lived, where they held lands, with details such as a sick grandfather coming to live with a family, or an elderly relative taking in a young niece as a companion. It is possible to see bare names on a family tree and to know that person x will certainly not be sitting down to dinner with person y.

The sort of information that can be found includes:

- Description of family relationships over several generations.
- Clarification of relationship between people of the same name.
- Drawings of family tree.
- Mortgages.
- Marriage settlements.
- Wills.
- Annuities with value ranging from just a few pounds a year to thousands.
- Dates of marriage and death, and very occasionally of birth.
- Accounts relating to land.
- Accounts relating to wills.
- Lists of assets – personal, household, farming, lands.
- Lists of tenants and rents paid.
- Names and descriptions of property.
- Value of property.
- Occupations.
- Confirmation of being overseas.
- Education of children under 21.
- Business records.
- Borough and town history.

The Bills and Answers, otherwise known as the Pleadings, which form the bulk of the records in the courts of equity, are the most useful type of document, containing the most information that will be relevant to a family historian, a local historian, a biographer and a social historian.

Reading the plaintiff's Bill of Complaint will almost certainly evoke your sympathy as you hear how badly he has been treated by other members of the family or by people he thought he could trust. Your sympathy will, however, remain only until you read the defendant's answer, and you suddenly realise that there is rather more to the case, and that perhaps your sympathy was rather too quickly given.

Local historians can use the records of the courts of equity to find details on when a house was built or rebuilt, particularly if money was borrowed to build it. Very occasionally there will be a description of the rooms of a house as in an inventory. Field names are often given, sometimes with the names of tenants and acreages and how the land was used. Where those bringing the case are wealthy the description of the land can extend over a whole manor or parish. Disputes over common land and tithes can give an insight into a locality.

Relationships Explained

The Bills and Answers provide some of the most useful information for confirming or explaining relationships, particularly when different generations of a family all have the same first names.

A case brought in 1718 between Francis Newman Esq. of North Cadbury, Somerset, Mary Gifford and John Hoskins Gifford is a good example of relationships being set out.[1] From this case we learn that Richard Newman of Fifehead Magdalen in Dorset died in September 1694, and that his eldest son Francis Holles Newman of North Cadbury died on 4 October 1714. By his wife Eleanor Mompesson he had the following children, and note that most of their dates of birth are very helpfully given:

Francis is aged over 21 in 1714
Thomas was born 23 March 1692
Richard was born 9 April 1693
Charles was born 14 May 1694
Henry was born 13 April 1696
John was born 5 May 1699, but died in his father's lifetime
William was born 14 November 1700
Eleanor was born 28 July 1703
Anne was born 14 September 1706

In addition we learn that Francis, the eldest son, married Dorothy Gifford who was brother to John Hoskins Gifford. In another related case we are told that Dorothy was the daughter of Mary and

Benjamin Gifford who married in about 1656.[2] After the death of her husband Benjamin Gifford, Mary married Hubert Hussey. Mary herself was the daughter of John Hoskins and Benjamin Gifford was the son of William Gifford who died on 26 September 1693.

In a drawn-out case in the 1830s, involving several documents and references, we learn that Lydia Robinson was still alive aged about 93, and head of a large family. The family were not particularly inventive with names so, we find:

Samuel son of Lydia
Samuel son of William who was son of Lydia
Samuel son of Thomas who was son of Lydia
Samuel son of John who was son of Lydia

In the same family we find:

Thomas son of Lydia
Thomas son of Thomas who was son of Lydia
Thomas son of Samuel who was son of Lydia

Women and Children as Parties to a Case
The courts of equity are one of the few sources of information where women have pretty much equal standing with men. In a simple case of debt a woman trading in goods such as silks might claim repayment of a debt in a court of equity. In more informative cases, a woman who does not feel she has received her rightful dowry may bring a case against her own father, or more often against his executors or his heirs after his death. If women are married their husbands are usually named, which means that a family of sisters claiming their dowries will all be named with their husbands.

The names of wives are often given in Chancery cases which can help identify particular families, especially when many have the same name. Looking again at the Robinson family case of the 1830s we find:

Lydia daughter of Lydia married Mr Betts
Janetta Betts married William Fanthorpe
Mary daughter of Samuel who was son of Lydia married
  Thomas Riley
Elizabeth daughter of Samuel who was son of Lydia remained
  a spinster
Eliza daughter of John who was son of Lydia married Thomas
  Maltby
Mildred daughter of John who was son of Lydia married
  William Jessop
Lydia daughter of Robert who was son of Lydia married
  Thomas Clater, and her sister married Henry Clater
Caroline daughter of Robert who was son of Lydia married
  Kington Pepper
Elizabeth daughter of Lydia married Mr Gilliat
Elizabeth Gilliat married John Whitton
Ann Gilliat married Robert Ireland

Wills Quoted
One of the principal benefits of studying the records of the courts of
equity is that a case will often revolve around a dispute over a will,
with the relevant parts being quoted. The cases usually involve the
executors and perhaps one of the beneficiaries in a dispute with
other beneficiaries.

The catalogue entries are often sufficiently detailed to give an
indication that a will is the subject of a case brought to a court of
equity, such as:

C 11/403/15
Plaintiffs: Jane Hoblyn, widow, Thomas Hoblyn, John Hoblyn,
John Harvey and Alice Harvey his wife, Jonathan Peter and
Mary Peter his wife (said Jane Hoblyn, together with Thomas
Hoblyn senior, who was father of said Thomas Hoblyn, John
Hoblyn, Alice Harvey and Mary Peter, were executrix of John
Hoblyn Esq. deceased which said Thomas and John Hoblyn

the sons, Alice and Mary are administratrix of said Thomas Hoblyn their father *with the will annexed*) creditors of estate of William Cary Esq. deceased, Charles Davy Esq., Robert Incledon Esq.
Defendants: Elizabeth Cary and John Hicks.

Wills proved abroad can often end up as Exhibits to a Chancery case such as:

C 111/75
Description:
SYME v LEE CORAGGIO v LEE: Weston's estate.
Includes: Exemplification of will (proved at Calcutta Supreme Court) of John Weston, a Lieutenant Colonel in the service of the United Company of Merchants of England, trading to the East Indies, 1819; *copy will and probate* of Phipps Weston, doctor in divinity of Henstridge, Somerset, 1777–1778
Date: 1842

Deeds, Leases, Trust Deeds, Mortgages
Locating deeds can be a difficult task for both family and local historians, and there is always a good chance that the ones that would give the information you are seeking no longer exist. The courts of equity can be a wonderful substitute as many deeds are recited in the Pleadings.

In 1824 Thomas Criddle of Wiveliscombe in Somerset, a tailor and draper, was admitted as a tenant to two cottages in North Street in Wiveliscombe 'commonly called The Bear Inn' to be held to his own use and also to the use of William Hancock the younger and John Hancock for the term of their lives at a yearly rent of 4s. 8d. and for a heriot of the best beast or goods with a proviso that William Hancock the younger should take no profit or advantage whilst the plaintiff lived, and that John Hancock should take no profit or advantage whilst William Hancock the younger lived. In 1825 a lease is recited whereby Thomas Criddle grants the two cottages which had recently been rebuilt to Christopher Harding for ninety-eight years, subject to the lives of the plaintiff, John and William Hancock. In 1839 the Bear Inn was mortgaged for £400. The Bear was then the subject of a marriage settlement and other mortgages and transfers, which are also quoted in the Chancery case which eventually ensued in 1842.[3]

A case of 1751 follows a similar thread, with a house and six closes of land being transferred from one person to another.[4] The case shows that the plaintiff Margaret Harris claims to be entitled to an annuity arising from the house and lands which had been bequeathed to her brother in their mother's will. Since the death of her brother and her brother's wife, this annuity has not been paid to her and she claims that Robert Lane, John Trewman and his wife Tryphena Trewman, who are now in the possession of these buildings and land, are required to pay her arrears and the annuity but that they refuse to do so. Deeds are quoted showing the descent of the land:

> Margaret Faggot
> To her son Mark Barton
> To his wife Sarah her executor Robert Lane then to
> To their son Mark Barton jun
> Sold to William Bradford 1740
> To wife Tryphena
> To her new husband John Trewman
> Mortgaged to John Stoodly Grant in trust for Mary and Jane
>   Trewman
> To Susanna Kelly widow
> To John Kelly her son (solicitor of plaintiff)

One of the principal reasons for bringing a case to an equity court rather than to a common law court is that the relevant documents have been lost, or are held by the other party. In these instances, the plaintiff will often quote what he believes to be the relevant part of a deed, and asks the defendant to corroborate or deny this by producing the document in court.

Cases frequently revolve around transactions relating to land. A simple case might just be a mortgage that has not been redeemed. Many are much more complicated, and are therefore full of much more interesting information. One of the most common types of case is one where the plaintiff believes that land was entailed a few generations earlier, and that he is the rightful heir under the entail. The defendant argues that there never was an entail and that the land was left by bequest in a will to someone else, from whom it has descended to the defendant. Cases involving mortgages can also be more interesting particularly if money was lent with land that was entailed being given as security. When the mortgagee tries to take possession of the land if his loan has not been repaid, he finds that he cannot as a third person claim that it is rightfully his under an entail, and that the mortgagor had no right to give this land as security. Where land has been entailed, or is believed to have been entailed, there will usually be a recital of all the generations following the original entail. Where the main male line has died out this can lead to interesting cases where the son of a younger son might claim that he has right to land which has been possessed by the daughter of an elder son. The actual wording of the entail, if indeed there ever was one, can be the only way of sorting this out, and again many generations will be described. These sorts of cases are the bread and butter of the courts of equity as they are more concerned with who possesses a piece of land, and thus receives the income from it, rather than who the legal ultimate owner might be.

In some cases a person will have leased out the land that is in dispute and here we can find the tenants and the field names all being given. For local historians this is invaluable information, and family historians might find the mention of an ancestor as tenant of a piece of land, even if the family were not thought to be of the social standing to bring a case to court themselves.

Recital of Several Generations

In many cases the source of the dispute can be many generations earlier than the date of the case.

One of the most difficult aspects of family history can be proving that one person is the son/daughter of the people you have reason to believe are their parents. A parish register might include a baptism that appears to be in the right place at the right time. This might perhaps be corroborated by a reference in a manorial court roll showing that the same piece of land was held first by the person who is believed to be the father, and then by the person who is believed to be the son. A case in an equity court can give proper proof of this, with several generations being named and described, crucially with both names and relationships given. Thus, a case often starts with a description of land held many years before, sometimes as many as 100, by 'my great grandfather'. The subsequent generations are then named and described. In a particularly useful case, the brothers, sisters, husband and wives will all be named and described for several generations.

A good example of this is to be found in the case brought by Francis Burgoyne against William Burgoyne and others in 1704.[5] In this Francis claims that William Burgoyne left a will in 1621 in which he bequeathed everything to his brother Robert Burgoyne. Robert then died in 1628 having left everything to his eldest son George who had been forced to flee the country as a Roman Catholic recusant. Before leaving the country George granted his lands to his brother in trust for his children. In typical Chancery case fashion, Robert Burgoyne the defendant claims that this is not true, and that in fact before going abroad George and his wife Helen sold all his lands to his younger brother Robert outright, and that there was no question of a trust. William the defendant is the son of this Robert who died in 1657 when the lands passed to his son William who therefore believes that he holds the lands. Along the way we find that George and his brother Robert also had brothers Richard, William and Philip and that Richard had a son Robert who in turn had a son Robert who ended up in prison.

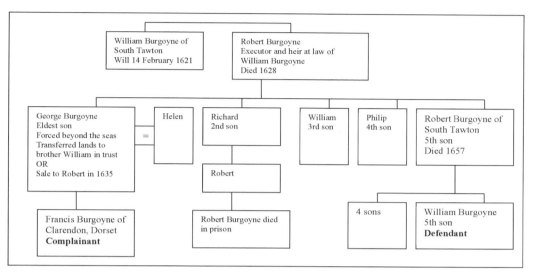

Another example is the case between John Lowe and members of the Moxon family. The Bill of Complaint in a case brought by John Lowe against Richard Moxon, Mary Moxon, Thomas Moxon, Nathaniel Moxon and Thomas Lowe does not survive.[6] However, there are several Answers dated 1808 to 1815 which give us plenty of information, going back four generations.

The case starts by reciting that in 1757 Thomas Lowe died, and that his brother Christopher was the executor of his will. In 1800 Thomas's son Richard Lowe of Little Over Co. Derby died leaving a will, and it is this will which is the subject of the dispute. Thomas left two children: Richard Lowe of Berache Heathcote who married without his father's consent and then died before his father, and Mary who married Richard Moxon, a currier. Mary had also died by the time the case came to court. Both Richard Lowe and Mary Moxon had children, who are of course great-grandchildren of Thomas Lowe who died in 1757:

Thomas Lowe
Mary Lowe

John Lowe
Richard Moxon
Mary Dawes
Thomas Moxon
Joseph Moxon
Nathaniel Moxon

In this case, Richard Moxon the eldest son of Mary and Richard Moxon has taken upon himself the care of not just his brothers and sisters, but also of the children of his uncle Richard Lowe (his mother's brother). The case is brought by John Lowe and Mary Lowe, Richard Lowe's children, against all the other children, particularly Richard Moxon who has spent a lot of the available money from Richard Lowe's estate in bringing up and educating the children. John Lowe claims that as residuary beneficiary of Richard Lowe's estate, there will be very little left for him.

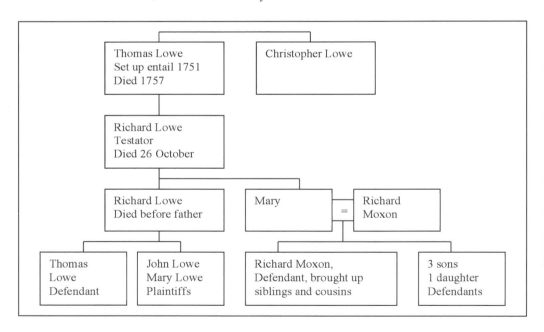

This case is typical for Chancery in that you see real human lives being lived out. When both Richard Lowe's children died, his grandson Richard Moxon stepped in to care for their children and to act as executor of his grandfather's will. We learn that he left his business as a cabinet maker and joiner in Derby to live with these younger children and to look after them. He has maintained his grandfather's farm as best he can, and believes that it is now in a better state than in his grandfather's lifetime. He has apprenticed his cousin, John Lowe, to a watchmaker in London. His own younger brother, Joseph, has been a soldier in the East Indies (and as he has not been heard of for seven years is no longer a defendant in the case). Thomas Lowe the eldest son is now farming the land. We also hear that they lived with their grandfather until the autumn of 1801.

Description of Interior of House

In 1667 there was a dispute over the White Hart inn in Wimborne, Dorset in which Mary the widow of the landlord, Reginald Speed, married William Harris in about 1663 and granted the inn to her new husband thus disinheriting her children.[7] She then died in 1666 and Thomas Speed and the other Speed children bring the case against William Harris. William is angry that Thomas Speed broke into the inn and has taken possession. Amongst other things we are given a description of the inside of the house with its furnishing:

> In the hall a table board two plank table boards, in the parlour two red serge cushions a livery cupboard a cupboard cloth two leather chairs.
> In the buttery one beer horse, in the kitchen one table board and form one plank form and shelves.
> In the chamber over the hall one joined table board and frame four joined stools one tester bedstead one trundle bedstead with bed mats and cords.
> In the chamber over the parlour and buttery one table board with a frame and one joined form, one livery cupboard

The White Hart, Wimborne.

and cupboard cloth, four leather chairs, one standing tester bedstead with curtains and valence, one trundle bedstead two feather beds two feather bolsters one flock bolster one rug one coverled three blankets and mats and four serge cushions.

In the chamber over the kitchen one table board and form one joined form one standing bedstead and one feather bed one feather bolster one coverled and a pair of blankets and a bed mat and cored.

In the little room over the staircase one table board and frame and in the chamber over the entry one tester bedstead with a cord and mat with several other goods which this defendant does not now remember, which said goods the complainant Thomas Speed has hitherto detained kept and converted to his own use

Thomas Speed has taken possession of these, as having previously been his mother's, but William Harris claims this is by force and that everything should belong to him.

Financial Standing

Some families who are involved in Chancery cases are, as would be expected, wealthy. Others are not. In 1657 there is a case concerning the estate of Edith Roberts, a widow, of Wilton in Wiltshire. Edith had two sisters Amy and Elizabeth.[8] Amy married Thomas Smith and had a daughter Edith who brings the case, with her husband John Smith. Elizabeth married John Woodroffe and had a daughter Mary. John Woodroffe is the defendant. This is really a fight between Edith's two nieces Edith and Mary.

According to Edith the plaintiff, her aunt had left all her personal belongings to her, 'linen, woollen, brass, pewter, bedding' and other things from the house, as she had looked after her aunt when she was ill.

According to Edith, her aunt also had £5 which had been put out to interest with a Mr Matthews and this was to be shared between the nieces Edith and Mary.

Edith claimed that her uncle John Woodroffe had come to the house and taken the household goods whilst Edith was 'out of doors'. He had also given Edith two bills of debt owing to him for £5 and said that Edith could claim them, but that she could not have the £5 with Mr Matthews. Edith is claiming the rest of the personal estate and her half of the £5 with Mr Matthews.

The defendant's Answer shows that there is another side to this. John Woodroffe says that actually Edith Roberts left the household goods to be divided equally between the two girls Edith and Mary, and the whole of the £5 to her daughter Mary. He does not know whether Edith spent her whole time looking after her aunt in her sickness, but it 'does not concern him'. He only took the household goods that Edith had thrown out, as this was Mary's share.

More commonly there are hundreds of pounds at stake, rather than the modest £5 in the above case.

A description in a document of someone as a yeoman, or a gentleman, or a merchant give some idea of their financial standing. An inventory with a will can also give some idea of wealth at the time of death, but usually only goods and chattels and not lands. The records of the courts of equity can give very much more detail on the social and financial standing of both a family and an individual person, as the cases brought to court include so much information on land holdings, dowries, debts, mortgages and the value of a deceased person's real and personal estate.

Details of Where a Family Lived

People are not always to be found living where you expect them. Elias Peck of Taunton Magdalen Co. Somerset, an apothecary, had a daughter Susannah to whom he left £40 in his will. According to the plaintiff, her husband, Susannah was under age when her father died, but she had been trained by her father in 'the art and mystery of an apothecary'.[9] Elias died thirty years before the case was brought to Chancery in 1709. After her father's death Susannah continued to work as an apothecary, however she then married Elias Ellis of Polterra Co. Cornwall who worked as an engineer in a tin works. Instead of moving to Cornwall with her new husband, Susannah remained in Taunton for fifteen years with her mother who said that she was quite incapable of managing the apothecary business without Susannah's help. In 1695 her mother died, and then

Susannah herself died, presumably without ever moving to Cornwall, but having left a will and appointing executors to her estate. Elias Ellis then felt that he had a claim on Susannah's estate, including asking for £20 for each of the years that Susannah lived with her mother. To Elias's displeasure Susannah's executors, John Kirkpatrick, John Amory, a grocer, and William Coles, a fuller, all of Taunton, took possession of her estate before Elias could travel from Cornwall to Taunton.

As so often in Chancery the defendant puts quite a different light on the story and claims that when Elias Peck made his will Susannah was already over 21 and married. They also say that her mother Johan was 'well skilled in the trade of an apothecary and understood the business without the assistance of Susannah', but that Susannah remained at home rather than moving to Cornwall with her husband because she was 'a weak infirm sickly and decrepit woman' who was not capable of doing or performing any servile business or labour. She complained that her husband was very unkind to her and was 'in very poor and mean circumstances' and could not maintain her. So it appears that she did indeed spend most, if not, all her life in Taunton, rather than moving to Cornwall with her husband.

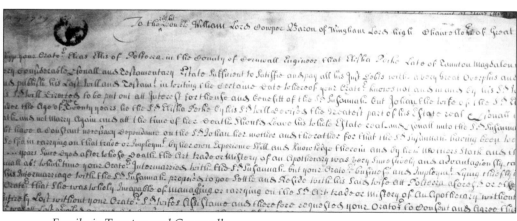

Family in Taunton and Cornwall.

Details of Business Transactions

The movements of goods for merchants often form the basis of equity court cases, whether to Europe or America, as a very common type of dispute is over the supposed disappearance of a cargo that was being shipped for sale, either to or from England. Quite detailed business transactions are included in some cases that are brought to court, where these are then the subject of a dispute.

In 1713 Samuel Avila, William Selleck and Thomas Perriam, all merchants in London, were joint owners of a ship called the *Mary Galley* and hired Samuel Ingram as master to take the ship to Cadiz in Spain and then on to Le Havre in France. However, Samuel Ingram remained in Cadiz and is now being asked to produce accounts.[10]

Not only English people were involved in Chancery cases. In the early eighteenth century we find that Peter Guenon de Beaubuisson, a merchant of London who was formerly a French merchant and who had left France suddenly because of his religion, was arrested for business debts owed to the defendants Simon Garnier and Elias Aubin, gentleman, although he claimed he had paid them all.[11]

In addition to merchants, many companies were involved in Chancery cases. A look at the catalogue for cases concerning companies in Manchester includes the following:

Reference: C 13/721/26
Document type: Two Bills and Answer.
Plaintiffs: Thomas Bolton of London, coal merchant.
Defendants: Jonathan Fisher, Roger Fisher and John James all of Liverpool Lancashire.
One answer not identified.
Subject: business deals between Thomas Bolton as agent for William Wilson and William Kirkby of Manchester, Lancashire, American merchants and the defendants along with John Fisher trading as Jonathan Fisher and Company, merchants and ship builders and Jonathan Fisher and Company, ship blacksmiths.
Date: 1818.

Reference: C 13/1172/20
Description:
Dearden v Manchester and Leeds Railway Company. Bill and three Answers.
Date: 1838.

Reference: C 13/2385/37
Description:
Manchester Bolton and Bury Canal Navigation and Railway Company v Gray. Bill only.
Date: 1835.

There are also many cases concerning the East India Company dating from the early seventeenth century. A typical entry from the catalogue reads:

Reference: C 6/407/44
Plaintiffs: Thomas Ekines merchant of London.
Defendants: New East India Company, [unknown] Catchpole factor and Peter Sherston ship's master.
Subject: Redress for the seizure of the plaintiff's ship the Ekines frigate by an East India Company factor. According to the plaintiff the ship was licensed to trade in the East Indies and had picked up a cargo of negroes to trade for pepper: Batavia, Jakarta, Java, East Indies; Achin, Atjeh, Indonesia, East Indies and property in Sumatra, Indonesia, East Indies.
Document type: Bill, Answer, Schedule.
Date: 1704.

Equally, there are a good number of records concerning people who served in India

Reference: C 16/306/T83
Cause number: 1865 T83.
Short title: In the matter of the estate of Ralph Thorpe major

in HM Indian Army in the Bengal establishment, barrack master, Dinapore, deceased: Crowder v de Brisay.
Documents: Administration summons.
Plaintiffs: Revd Augustus Edward Crowder, Anna Maria Bowne Crowder his wife and other infants by Augustus Edward Crowder their next friend.
Defendants: Henry De La Cour de Brisay.
Date: 1865.

Anyone studying business history would ignore the records of the courts of equity at their peril.

Bearing in mind that loans of money for business purposes, as for personal reasons, came from friends and family, it is not unusual for business loans to be the subject of a case in the courts of equity.

In 1673 Walter Wakeley of Bridport, a beer brewer, needed to borrow some money, so he talked to his 'pretended friend' Thomas Snook of Dorchester, a maltster. Snook in turn borrowed £30 from Mr Perkins of Martins Town, giving him 'some small security'.[12] In his Bill of Complaint Walter Wakeley claims that Thomas Snook then combined with William Maris of Bridport, a tallow chandler, who said that the safest way for Snook to secure his loan was by a mortgage of a tenement that belonged to Wakeley in the borough of Bridport, valued at £5 p.a. This was duly set up and the security given. However, the loan of £30 was never made, although demands for repayment were made. And 'more injuriously', Snook caused Wakeley to be arrested unless he would give bail of £500 and he feared he would 'lie and perish' in Dorchester gaol. Snook then points out that there had been a long series of loans to Wakeley over a lengthy period, and the mortgage agreement was to cover all these.

There are a huge number of cases relating to companies, particularly railway and banking companies. Typical entries taken from Calendar of Orders and Decrees, 1869 include reference to:

Barneds Banking Co.
Warrington Wire Rope Company
Vestry of St Giles, Camberwell
Blakeley Ordnance Company
British & American Telegraph Company
Birmingham Banking Company
Beariz Tin Streaming Company
Brampton and Longtown Railway Company
Bristol Soap and Trading Company
India Rubber Gutta Percha Company

Another case that evokes an emotional response came to the Court of the Star Chamber in 1606 and involves the Farwell family of Holbrook in Somerset, although in this case I am not sure that we feel much sympathy for any of the people involved except perhaps the elderly father who watches his warring sons. It all starts with the death of John Copleston who gave his wife and children legacies amounting to £4,500.

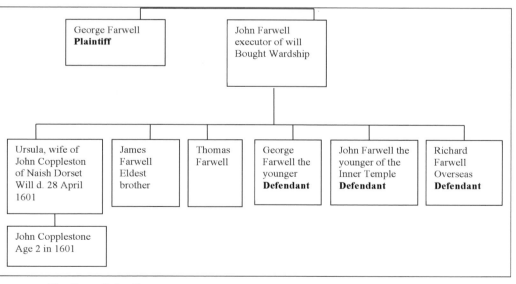

The Farwell family tree.

John Copleston's son and heir John was an infant, so John Farwell the elder of Holbrook, grandfather, was appointed as overseer and executor. Some of John Copleston's lands were held in chief, so the king is entitled to wardship of the child and to the lands. As was the custom then, John Farwell the elder bought the wardship for £220. His sons Richard, George the younger and John the younger (sons of John the elder) decided to defraud John the elder of this right.

In this case, we hear that Richard was 'lovingly entertained' by his father at Holbrook. With the help of John the younger at the Inner Temple who was 'of a very malicious disposition and once put out of the house of the Inner Temple in 1601' he broke into the study and chest with counterfeit keys and took the deeds to London, saying that he would make his brother James 'the poorest hare in Somerset' and plotted to take the documents overseas to Spain.

Their father aged three score years and twelve (72) was in 'great danger and peril of his life and was in an extremity of grief and sorrow over this'. Richard Farwell then wrote a letter of apology to his father:

> fortune has possessed me with divers papers and receipts of accounts which were in your custody intending to ship them with me yet then for Spain if not thither then to some other land as foreign where for your safety and security I will keep them so secret that no English eye will see them being, Sir, without intention to arm myself with any pretended title against your possessions for I call to witness heavens all seeing eye that my heart wishes you a long quiet and peaceable life

Then there was the incident at Holbrook with James Farwell the eldest brother, who was abiding in his father's house at Holbrook and not suspecting any outrage or violence. Meanwhile, Richard, George the younger and John the younger arrive 'with malicious hatred to their elder brother James' and in July or August last year:

A line drawing of Holbrook House.

in very riotous and forceable manner assemble themselves together at Holbrook arrayed with rapiers daggers and other weapons both invasive and defensive and they the said riotous persons being so assembled together did at the time aforesaid in like riotous and unlawful manner and weaponed as aforesaid did come and enter into an inner part in their father's house at Holbrook

James and his father were in the inner parlour, and in the presence of their father, Richard, John and George most irreverently and in a barbarous manner and irreverently railed at their eldest brother James:

then and there in like barborous riotous and violent manner in the presence of the father did assault and beat and wound him their eldest brother and with their daggers drawn in their hands cadging and swearing by many fearful and horrible oaths that they said riotous and disordered persons would stab and kill their said eldest brother

Father was badly affected by this:

he their said father kneeling upon his knees to his riotous and unnatural sons besought them to be pacified and to desist from that their ungodly and unnatural attempt being stricken with such an amazement at such unexpected violence offered in his presence as with the terror and fear thereof he being an aged man was almost at the point of death

In his Answer John Farwell the younger makes us look at the case with slightly different eyes. He believes that the case has been brought because of the rancour and uncharitable revengefulness of James Farwell and Thomas Farwell who have incited their uncle the plaintiff George the elder who is acting 'out of an unnatural bitterness and evident envy'. James and Thomas persuaded their father to withhold John the younger's allowance and he has not received any payment for his livelihood and maintenance for two years. John agrees that the bonds and deeds were taken by Richard Farwell but it has nothing to do with him. One of the bonds of John Copleston was granted in his will to Richard Farwell, however on learning that the bonds that Richard had taken did not include the one he had been thus granted, John the younger returned one of the bonds that he had taken back to his father. James and Thomas accused John the younger of taking them and had him put in the Fleet Prison. None of the bonds was found and he was released and the deeds were returned by Richard to the father. Originally the father had asked John the younger to deal with the Court of Wards, and he got on with this, but he was hindered by the baby's mother Ursula.

In answer to the claim by Thomas and James that they thought that John the younger was trying to defraud the family and wanted a Mr Parsons to take over, John the younger says that he did indeed write a letter, but it just said that he would agree to Mr Parsons taking over.

In response to the accusation that John the younger was accused of being thrown out of the Inner Temple, he says that in fact, seven or eight years ago, at the age of 20, he and Francis Tresham got into a fight in a field near Lincoln's Inn because Tresham made disparaging speeches about John's father. Out of love and duty for his father he defended his father's name. Tresham assaulted and wounded him with his rapier and dagger, and having lost a lot of blood he fought back, but then Tresham was joined by three or four of his company armed with pistols and swords. After the fight, John went into dinner at the Inner Temple house and thought he was free of violence but Tresham came in and struck and stabbed John with a dagger. Tresham was instantly expelled, and John was asked not to come into the house, but was never expelled from his chambers.

It was alleged that Richard, John the younger and George the younger assembled in riotous and forcible manner in Holbrook and would have killed James if their father hadn't been almost dead from the 'amazement' of it all. In response John the younger says that actually George the younger was going to marry Margaret Johnson and John the elder, his father, had promised him a sum of money. James didn't like this and accused George of 'being his natural brother both by father and mother of bastardy'. John junior tried to persuade George to ignore it, but James continued to plot and involved his brother Thomas, 'a man known according to the portion of his capacity to be a secret contriver of sundry scandals infamies and slanders the cancour of covetousness having so far eaten into and possessed their dispositions as having neither fear or feeling of the world's censure or their one shame'. Richard was going to be granted a rectory by his father, but James didn't like this either and continued the bastardy rumour.

Richard, John the younger and George the younger went to Holbrook to ask James to repeat his accusation in front of their father in the inner parlour. They did not go armed, though John the younger admits he did have a 'little dagger at his back which he did daily wear both then and before that time'. James slandered their mother although she had been dead some twenty years, and had had a good name for fifty years.

They tested the patience of John the younger, but the father sided with James and Thomas and we have already heard that John the younger was deprived of his maintenance and then put in the Fleet Prison. Oh, the joys of families! And what a resource for researchers!

WHAT SORT OF INFORMATION MIGHT BE FOUND IN A BUNDLE OF DEPOSITIONS?

Depositions are the statements by witnesses given in support of the cases put by the plaintiffs and defendants. The plaintiff and defendant each prepared a list of questions, known as Interrogatories, and the deponents (witnesses) who were chosen by the plaintiff and defendant then answered as many questions as were appropriate.

It is worth noting that there is only one list of Interrogatories on behalf of the plaintiff, and one on behalf of the defendants, so they have to be worded to include all the information that any of the deponents might give. This means that the deponents do not all answer every single question.

One of the great benefits arising from the Depositions is the fact that a huge variety of people were asked to give evidence. On the documents, each deponent's name, age, occupation and place of abode are given before the actual answers to the questions. This means that the deponents are of interest, particularly for family historians, for their own sake as well as for the information they bring to bear on the case. In some cases the age is exact, in some it is approximate and in some it just states that the person is over 21. The place of abode is of course a great help to family historians, as it can pinpoint a person to a particular place at a particular time. Generally one of the questions will ask for information about how long the deponent has lived in the place, or how long they have known the parties to the case. This of course will elicit such information as the fact that they have lived in the parish for say thirty years but lived for the previous twenty years in 'x' parish where they were born.

The list of questions, or Interrogatories, can cover many pages, particularly if there are a great many deponents all with slightly different information to offer. Sometimes there are just a few questions which are asked of only two or three deponents, such as whether you were the witness to a will.

Cases in the courts of equity almost seemed designed to pull on the heart strings. They are full of stories of people being mistreated, most often by the closest members of their families.

A case of 1721 relating to the Slaney family is a good example.[13] This case concerns the fate of the younger children of John Slaney, and whether or not James Crump as executor of the will had looked after the farm properly and spent the money on the children in a way that befitted their deceased father's social standing.

John Slaney died on Christmas Day 1699, and his wife Elizabeth died about a month later in February 1700, leaving six children, around whom the case revolves. When their parents die, the eldest child is 10, the youngest '¼ year old'. Five of the children are plaintiffs (John, Elizabeth, Lydia, Sarah and Hannah), and the primary defendant is James Crump, the sole executor of the parents' wills. The sixth child (Mary) is a also defendant. The plaintiffs (now much older – it is 1721) claim that their uncle James Crump has:

- Misused and abused their father's large estate, using ready money and property/profits for his own benefit. They claim he had/has a large amount of money coming in from rents, arrears of rent, debts owed etc.
- Has treated them harshly and poorly, paying insufficiently towards their maintenance and education, and sending them into apprenticeships and into service when they were too young (one aged 14).
- James Crump has conned them in various ways: he has misled them about the size of the real and personal estate (including waiting too long for the appraisement, which was

finally carried out in June 1700) which then grossly undervalued the estate; has tricked them into accepting only a £150 legacy each when they reached 21, rather than the £500 each that they were entitled to. Not only this, but James Crump tricked them into signing a general release; they believed these were just acknowledging the receipt of the £150 but in fact it acknowledged they were not entitled to anything else out of the estate. At first they were 'unable to undergo the expense of a suit to call him to account and being unwilling to think that the said Crump who was so near a relation would have attempted to wrong them'.

• They argue they have since learnt from sources that the estate was much bigger, and they deserve much more money than this, but they can produce no one to consolidate their claims (their parents are dead, other people who could possibly testify are abroad).

• They claim Crump refuses to show them accounts or give them any more money.

• They ask the court to overturn the releases and for Crump to give them their deserved money.

Crump responds first with a plea claiming that the releases that were signed (which he can produce) effectively nullify the bill altogether. He then goes on to answer the questions anyway, arguing that he has neither been deceitful nor negligent.

He claims that there were debts to cover, lots of maintenance to pay, the leasehold properties actually lost him money, that the £150 legacy to each child was generous and that the estate is just not as big as they believe. He claims he has lost out as executor and explains that the appraisement took an extra few months because there was smallpox in the family.

These orphaned children believed that they came from a reasonably well-to-do family, and should have each received £500 which would have provided a good education and clothes befitting their station in life.

The really good information in this case comes from the Interrogatories and Depositions. The list of Interrogatories for the plaintiffs starts with the question:

> Do you know the parties, complainants and defendant in the title of this Interrogatory mentioned any or either or which of them. If yea, how long have you so known them respectively and did you know John Slaney late of Staplehurst in the County of Kent Yeoman and Elizabeth his wife both deceased, late father and mother of the complainants John Slaney, Elizabeth, Lydia, Sarah and Hannah; if yea, how long did you know them before their deaths and when did they respectively die as you know or have heard and believe declare.

The answers to this first question can often be some of the most useful, as they can indicate how long the deponent has been living in the parish. If he replies that he has known the parties all his life, the implication is that he was born in the parish, if he has only known them a few years, then it is likely that he came from elsewhere.

There then follow another twelve questions, concerning the state of the farm during the lifetime of John Slaney the father, and what the rents were, whether or not there was any timber and what it was worth, what the inventory of John Slaney's estate showed, and what it was worth. There are then questions aimed at those who owed money to John Slaney at the time of his death and those to whom he owed money. These are followed by the questions that shed the most light on the family as people and about the education and maintenance of the children. One of the last questions asks in what manner John Slaney was buried and what the funeral charges were.

Depositions in this case were given by a large number of people:

John Lamb of Shadoxhurst in the county of Kent, clerke, aged about 46 years

Henry Littleale of Biddenden in the county of Kent, yeoman, aged 50 years and upwards

Thomas Hon of Cranbrooke in the county of Kent,
  clothworker, aged 60 years and upwards
William Greenhill of Linton in the county of Kent, yeoman,
  aged about 54 years
Edward Knell of Staplehurst in the county of Kent,
  husbandman, aged 45 years or thereabouts
Joseph Butcher of Headcorn in the County of Kent,
  husbandman, aged 66
Robert Love of Staplehurst in the county of Kent, gentleman,
  aged 49 years or thereabouts
Martha Eaves, wife of George Eaves of Staplehurst in the
  county of Kent, gentleman, aged 44
Thomas Young of Staplehurst in the county of Kent, yeoman,
  aged 70 years or thereabouts
Hannah Osborne, wife of William Osbourne of Staplehurst in
  the county of Kent, gentleman, aged 50 years and upwards
John Hope of Maidstone in the county of Kent, butcher, aged
  43 years
John Knell of Cranbrooke in the county of Kent, yeoman, aged
  44 years
Joseph Stanley of Sutton Valence in the county of Kent,
  yeoman, aged 73 years and upwards
Thomas Rayner of Sutton Valence in the county of Kent,
  blacksmith, aged 33 years
John Crump of Staplehurst in the county of Kent, yeoman,
  aged about 35 years
Robert Browne of Maidstone in the county of Kent, linen
  draper, aged 3 and 40 years and upwards
Elizabeth Eves, wife of Thomas Eves of Headcorn in the
  county of Kent, husbandman, aged 50 years and upwards
Thomas Crump of Maidstone in the county of Kent, distiller,
  aged 30 years or thereabouts
Edward Reynolds of Staplehurst in the county of Kent,
  husbandman, aged 69 years or thereabouts
John Chaxfield of Staplehurst in the county of Kent, yeoman,
  aged 40 years

Elizabeth Jefferry, wife of Robert Jefferry of Staplehurst in the
county of Kent, cordwainer, aged 60 years and upwards
Ann Perse, wife of Edward Perse of Benenden in the county
of Kent, grazier, aged about 50 years
Catherine Edmett, wife of John Edmett of Staplehurst in the
county of Kent, aged 46 years and upwards
John Edmett of Staplehurst in the county of Kent, clothier,
aged 43 years or thereabouts

As can be seen, there is a good variety of occupations including a
cordwainer, distiller, linen draper, blacksmith and several
husbandmen. These records are particularly useful for information
on those of humble origins. It will also be noticed that women are
as likely to be deponents as men.

The detail to be found in the Depositions can be eye-opening.
The Depositions are full of little titbits of information, such as the
fact that Henry Littleale of Biddenden lived with John Slaney for
fourteen years before his death, and that the twenty-one-year lease
on the farm had just been renewed by John Slaney and was worth
£600. When discussing John Slaney's corn, William Greenhill tells
us that Slaney had so much corn that the usual barns and outhouses
were not sufficient to hold the harvest. William Greenhill also tells
us that he was employed by James Crump after he took over the farm
for seven years, and then goes on to say that the maintenance and
education of the children was not suitable considering the wealth
left by their parents. Although John Slaney, the eldest of the children,
was supposed to be brought up to understand farming, so that he
could take over the farm, in fact:

Crump put out the said complainant John Slaney first upon
liking to a country shop keeper and at last found him an
apprentice to a baker in London which in this deponent's
judgement was not suitable either to the intent of the
defendant Crump's trust or the ability of the said complainant
Slaney as then expected.

He goes on to say that James Crump kept all the daughters at home upon the said farm or at another farm of the said defendants and 'kept them there employed in work relating in part to the managing of the said farms and this deponent saith he hath several times seen the eldest daughter of the said John Slaney to lay bands to bind corn with and saith he this deponent taught the said Eldest Daughter to write and believes the said children were taught to read severally by dames'.

This, together with information from some of the other deponents, tells us that there was an elder daughter, Jane, who was from a first marriage, who was treated differently. She was taught to read by William Greenhill, a local yeoman, whereas the other children were taught to read and write at school. She was made to work on the farm rather than being apprenticed as the other children were. Once again, equity court cases lead one's imagination to work overtime. How did Jane feel about being treated differently? How did the other children act towards her?

The deponent Edward Knell tells us that John Slaney died of smallpox, which is presumably what also took away his wife so soon after, leaving the orphaned children. Concerning the upkeep of the poor orphans by their uncle, Hannah Osbourne tells us that:

> their maintenance was very plain and cheap and believes they wanted nothing as to sustenance but their clothing was very ordinary and consisting chiefly of Linsey Woolsey and coarse linen and not in any manner equal in goodness to the linen and clothing they usually had in the life time of their father and mother.

She tells us that she knows this as she was:

> a near neighbour to the said complainants and often saw them and considered these circumstances; and that the complainant Hannah being about a quarter of a year old at the death of her parents was put out to nurse at the next house to this deponent by her mother before her mother's decease.

John Crump, who has been called as a deponent by James Crump claims that far from the poor orphans being treated badly, they were treated well, and proceeds to tell us about each one:

> they were fed the same as his own children were, that they were well clothed and that they were all sent to school to learn to read and brought up like yeomen children of the country, except that the said plaintiff John Slaney had better learning him being at Maidstone one year and upwards of board where he learned to write better and learned arithmetic; And this deponent further saith that Elizabeth continued under the care and was educated, brought up and maintained by this deponent's father from her mother's death until she went to live with the widow Sharpish as a servant.

He tells us that Lydia, one of the daughters, was:

> Likewise brought up, maintained and educated from the death of her mother at the expense of his father James Crump the defendant until she went to live with her uncle Frensham; that John Slaney the plaintiff was likewise brought up, maintained and educated at the expense of his father the said defendant from the death of his said mother until he was put out as apprentice by his father to a baker in London at about his age of thirteen or fourteen years; that Mary was likewise brought up, maintained and educated at the expense of his father from the death of her said Mother until she was put out as apprentice to a mantua maker at Staplehurst where she continued some time and until she was put out as apprentice to a mantua maker at Smarden in the County of Kent; that Sarah was likewise educated, brought up and maintained at the expense of his father the said defendant from the death of her said Mother until she went to London to live, where after she having been about two or three years she married the plaintiff Beesley and was then about one and twenty; that the

61

said Hannah was likewise maintained, brought up and educated at the expense of this deponent's father the said defendant from the death of her mother until she was put out an Apprentice at London to a mantua maker.

Robert Browne, who also speaks for the defendant James Crump says that:

he had several times sold unto the said Defendant and unto his daughter who had the care of them several parcels of linen goods to make them frocks, aprons and handkerchiefs to the value of three and four pounds at a time, and had made out particular bills for their use and secured his money of the defendant.

Regarding their clothes, Elizabeth Eves says that they were: 'brought up at the expense of the said defendant James Crump in a handsome manner being kept tight in apparel tho' not in gaudy apparel'. Such detail about the lives of these young orphans is unlikely to come from any other source, and illustrates the richness of the courts of equity as a means of finding out more about the day-to-day lives of people, whether contented or struggling, and in particular the usefulness of the Interrogatories and Depositions.

HOW HELPFUL ARE THE EQUITY COURT RECORDS FOR ESTABLISHING THE ORIGINS OF EMIGRANTS?
America
Establishing the origins of emigrants abroad from England is notoriously difficult, but on occasion the records of the courts of equity can help. Cases relating to America date from the early seventeenth century, those for Europe from much earlier and those for Australia obviously much later. The most useful cases concerning America for family and local historians are those where there is a dispute over an estate in England, and one of those involved has moved to America or the West Indies. There are also

a large number of cases referring to merchants sailing to the Americas. Knowing of the interest in American emigrants, TNA's catalogue is generally quite good at identifying cases that include references to emigrants, such as an entry in the Court of Exchequer Depositions for 1731:[14]

> Herbert Jefferys, gent. v. Edward Lewis, gent., James Thomas, Thos. Lewis, Thos. Thomas, Henry Matthews and his wife Mary: Last will and testament, and the value, &c., of the estate of Thos. Edwards, sometime since of Kington (Hereford), but late of the parish of St. Anne, in the county of Essex, in the colony of Virginia in America, clerk; the estate including a capital messuage or tenement situate in Old Kington (Hereford).

In a case brought in 1731 a Philadelphia connection is proved as we learn that Humphrey Tompkins died seised of several lands, all of which were mortgaged for 500 years.[15] In his will he bequeathed these in trust to his brother-in-law Edward Browne and his son Edward Tompkins. However only Edward Tompkins acted as executor and having proved the will on 1 December 1687, he then left for America in 1700 and settled in Pennsylvania. Edward Tompkins left behind him three daughters, Anne, Martha and Mary, all infants at the time (there is no mention of their mother). When Edward Tompkins left for America, the holder of the mortgages, William Turbill, took possession of the properties, renting them out to other people named. The plaintiffs claim that initial mortgages have since been paid off by way of rent from the properties, and therefore the properties should return to the daughters, Anne and Martha (Mary sold her share to Anne's husband David Davis previously). It is interesting to note that Edward Tompkins supposedly left England because the lands were mortgaged, but actually the dates don't really match up. However, he did leave for America, abandoning his three infant daughters:

although your Orators said father Edward Tompkins sometime of the city of London but afterwards of Philadelphia aforesaid esquire did over about the first day of December which was in the year of our Lord 1687 duly prove the said will in common form yet it so happened that soon afterwards finding the said several estates to him devised encumbered with mortgages as in the said last will is mentioned and being inclined to travel and affecting to reside in foreign parts did in or about the year of our Lord 1700 transport himself from this kingdom to the province of Pennsylvania aforesaid and settled at and in Philadelphia and in the year of our Lord [blank] departed this life intestate and having issue only three children to witt your Orators Anne Davies, Martha Lloyd and their sister Mary Noyes hereinbefore names then all of very tender years and infants.

The ages of Edward Tompkins' daughters when he left for America (note especially how Mary is abandoned by her father and by her husband) are made clear:

your Orator Anne did not attain her age of 21 years until the 29th October 1715 be her marriage with your Orator David Davies hath been under coverture ever since 1719 and your Orator Martha did not attain her age of 21 years until 25th May 1718 and then and ever since was under coverture of her husband your Orator Walter Lloyd and the said Mary Noyes did not attain her age of 21 years until the 30th July 1714 and then was under coverture of John Noyes her late husband deceased and so continued till of late he having about 10 years since departed on a voyage to the West Indies and never been heard of since.

In addition to the Pleadings, there are many references to America in the Chancery Exhibits such as in the case Hayter v Hunt which includes a letter of attorney dated 1682 from the President and Fellows of Harvard College appointing John Richards in New England as attorney 'for the only proper use and benefit of the said College' within the Kingdom of England.[16] This is signed by John Rogers, and witnessed by James Whetcombe, Robert Johnson, Thomas Dolls and Increase Mather, and includes the Harvard seal embossed on the letter.

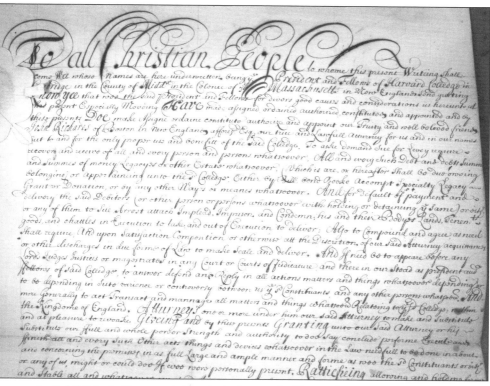

An Exhibit including appointment of attorney for Harvard.

Europe

Cases relating to Europe proliferate throughout the courts of equity, though most refer to merchants working abroad, rather than to emigrants. An early one dated 1475–85 relating to a debt that was paid in London is listed in the catalogue as:

C 1/60/7
Plaintiffs: Ambrose de Baraciis, of Italy.
Defendants: Everard Neuchirche, of London, pewterer.

A case in 1729 is listed in the catalogue as:

C 11/363/42
Plaintiffs: Francis Barnes, mercer and shopkeeper late of
London and now of Vineing, Germany and Henry Barnes,
innholder of Hastings, Sussex.
Defendants: Richard Weller and Henry May.

In 1803 a case is brought by two of the executors of the will dated
9 July 1778 of Alexander Livingston, a merchant in Rotterdam,
against the Bank of England.[17] In this case the parties are merely
seeking authorisation from the court, rather than being involved in
a real dispute. The money from Alexander Livingston's estate was
invested in annuities and other stock in the Bank of England. Two of
the executors have moved from Rotterdam to England and want the
accounts to be held in just their names, the third executor (and
widow of the testator) remaining in Rotterdam. The Bank asks for
direction from a court of equity before doing this.

Australia
A look at TNA's online catalogue shows that there are cases relating
to Australia such as one dated 1849:[18]

Plaintiffs: William Vardon and another.
Defendants: William Andrus, George Andrus, Henry Andrus
all of Sutton, Anne Andrus, Jane Andrus, Mordecai Fraser
Andrus, William Andrus of Brighton, George Andrus of
Richmond Street, James Andrus, George Tripp and Caroline
Tripp his wife (deleted), Harriet Ridley widow, Mana
Andrus, Francis Andrus, Patience Andrus, Henry Andrus
(abroad) of Australia (abroad) and Charles Andrus.

IS IT WORTH LOOKING – WHAT SORT OF PEOPLE HAD CASES HEARD IN A COURT OF EQUITY?

It is always worth looking, but there are some avenues of research that make success in finding useful information more likely. If a family historian is researching an unusual name, it is certainly worth a look at TNA's online catalogue which covers most of the basic Chancery pleadings and some of the Depositions. This is equally true if the surname being researched is common but only in a small localised area.

The most likely type of people to have been involved in an equity case will be people who owned something, be it land or money. Thus farmers, tradesmen, skilled artisans and their wives and families are likely to appear in the records. Even more likely are those described as 'gentleman'. In some settings this can refer to someone who is very well off, in other more rural areas it signifies someone who is little more than a yeoman farmer, but who holds some land that is then leased to others.

As a strict rule of thumb, if the family left wills, they are likely to be the sort of people to be involved in a case. This is not forgetting that rather humbler people are often called as deponents to answer Interrogatories.

If searching for an emigrant to America, it is always worth a look. The TNA online catalogue includes some references to cases that involve an emigrant, but by no means all are included.

Some of the classes of pleadings have been catalogued with place names, which can be of great value to local historians, however most of the indexes have been geared to personal names, so a local historian would have to have a good idea of the landowning families in the area being studied.

WHY DID SOMEONE TAKE A CASE TO AN EQUITY COURT?

As so many cases involve loans of money it is worth remembering that banks did not lend money in the modern sense, and that if someone needed money they applied to their friends and neighbours, and usually secured the loan with a mortgage of land. This sort of activity gave rise to a wonderful number of cases, full of details of both families and lands.

Cases involving what appear to be straightforward debts, such as not paying for goods, would normally be heard in the courts of common law, but these often come to the courts of equity when the correct documents are not to hand, or are being held by the other party. Many equity cases request an injunction to stop a common law case from proceeding, so that the case can then be heard in the equity court, where the plaintiff presumably feels he will receive a fairer hearing.

Children bring cases, represented by their 'next friend' when their inheritance is being threatened in some way. The inheritance can be for many thousands of pounds, or it can be very modest, but if there is a feeling that the eldest son is denying his younger sisters their rightful marriage portions, but spending the money that their father said was to be paid for them, then they will bring a case asking for full accounts to be presented to the court, showing that there was sufficient money for their marriage portions. Perhaps even more common than this type of case is the sort where an executor, or in some more complicated cases (but much more exciting and useful to the researcher) the executor of the executor of the executor of the original testator, is not managing the land and money properly and the children feel that their inheritance will be jeopardised.

There are a huge number of other reasons why a case can be brought. The variety of family feuds that end up in the courts of equity is almost unlimited. It seems to be a rule of nature that people do not always get on with other people and they particularly do not get on with family members and friends.

GEOGRAPHICAL JURISDICTION OF THE COURTS OF EQUITY

The main courts of Chancery and Exchequer had jurisdiction over the whole of England and Wales, as did the Court of the Star Chamber and the Court of Requests. The more local courts had a limited jurisdiction, but the widest of these is the Duchy of Lancaster with lands all over the country, the majority of which are in Lancashire, Yorkshire, Cheshire, Staffordshire and Lincolnshire, but there are lands in Somerset, Durham and Suffolk amongst others. There are also lands in London, particularly in the Savoy area. The Palatinate courts of Lancaster, Chester and Durham were generally restricted to their particular counties. The courts did not have jurisdiction over Scotland, but many cases involve people who lived or had property there. Typical entries in the catalogue read:

C 11/1344/5
Document type: Depositions.
Plaintiffs: James Gordon, merchant of Edinburgh, Scotland.
Defendants: John Cruickshanks Esq. and Richard Rigby, merchant of London.
Depositions taken at Edinburgh, Scotland.
Date: 1723.

C 13/602/1
Description:
[C1803 M1].
Short title: Macdonald v Campbell.
Document type: Bill and three Answers.
Plaintiffs: Hon Archibald Macdonald of Jermyn Street, St James Westminster, Middlesex and Jane Macdonald his wife (late Jane Campbell, spinster).
Defendants: Evan Baillie, Barbara Campbell, Sir John Sinclair bart of Ulbister, Caithness, Scotland, Sir John McGregor bart of Lunrick, Perthshire, Scotland, Murray Duncan Campbell Esq. of Edinburgh, Vans Hathorn Esq. of Edinburgh, Robert Gordon (abroad), William Alexander (abroad), James Campbell (abroad) and Donald Campbell (abroad).

Amended by an order dated 25 January 1803:

Sir John Sinclair bart of Ulbister, Caithness, Scotland,
Sir John McGregor bart of Lunrick, Perthshire, Scotland,
Murray Duncan Campbell Esq. of Edinburgh, Vans Hathorn
Esq. of Edinburgh removed as defendants and made
plaintiffs.
Original bill Easter 1798, plaintiffs name Baillie with
Mr Edmonstone (Reynardsons division).
Subject: payments due under the marriage settlement of
plaintiffs from the estates of Duncan Campbell in St Vincent
and Demerrer, West Indies.
Date: 1803.

Ireland was also not under the jurisdiction of the courts of equity,
but many cases concern the lands of English people in Ireland, and
where tenants are named, or deeds survive in the Exhibits, there is
a useful amount of information.

C 6/76/21
Plaintiffs: Roger Drake.
Defendants: Susannah Drake and Stephen White.
Subject: the Three Nuns [Inn], in Gutter Lane, London, and
property in Ireland.
Document type: Answer only.
Date: 1676.

C 6/312/30
Description:
Plaintiffs: Edward Browne.
Defendants: Robert Clayton and Peter Debilly.
Subject: insurance policies relating to the siege and fall of
towns in Ireland.
Document type: two Answers.
Date: 1699.

C 11/2425/8
Plaintiffs: Elizabeth [Hare] dowager Baroness of Coleraine in

Ireland, widow.
Defendants: Arthur Trevor Esq., Robert Edwards and
Elizabeth Somerfield.
Document type: Bill and Answer.
Date: 1730.

THE COSTS OF BRINGING A CASE

The costs relating to a case can be clarified in a variety of records.
The Masters' Reports are perhaps the most informative, as the
Masters were set the task of taxing the lawyers' costs. This
Deposition included accounts:[19]

Paid to John Langley for serving and making affidavits and serving subpoenas	£1 0s 0d
Paid for expenses at Warminster at a commission out of the court	£1 0s 0d
Paid to two commissioners for their pains	£2 0s 0d
For making the depositions and engrossing	6s 0d
Paid for expenses in execution of a commission at Wincanton issue of this court in these causes	£12 18s 6d

MEDIEVAL AND EARLY MODERN HISTORY

The courts of equity are particularly useful for students of late
medieval and early modern history. The records in the Court of
Chancery are reasonably well described in the catalogue and include
such gems as the case brought by Edward Baynton and his wife
Agnes in the period 1558–79 against Henry Baynton and his wife
Dorothy and Jane Marshall.[20] This case concerns a reviewing of a
previous case brought locally concerning the judgement accusing
Agnes Mylles of murder. Criminal cases do not feature in the courts
of equity, however this case is brought as there is an accusation of
perjury in the earlier case.

Agnes Mylles of Stanley Wiltshire, widow, apparently used
sorcerer's charms to murder William Baynton, the son and heir
apparent of the plaintiffs Edward and Agnes Baynton, on the Friday

before Palm Sunday 6 Elizabeth (1564). Agnes confessed to the murder but said that it was done by the 'enticement and procurement' of Dorothy wife of Henry Baynton, and was then hanged at Fisherton Co. Wiltshire. In this case it is important to realise that if Edward the plaintiff died without issue his lands would go in tail to Henry Baynton and his issue, whose wife 'procured' the murder. Henry and Dorothy now have three sons and two daughters and so are in a good position to inherit if Edward and Agnes should die childless. Jane Marshall is introduced into the case as she said she could detect people using witchcraft and so the plaintiffs had asked her in the original case to give evidence which she did. She said that Dorothy Baynton was the procurer of Agnes Mylles who committed the murder. Henry and Dorothy now say that Agnes was not guilty and want Jane to retract her evidence and have caused her to be imprisoned and will only have her released if she retracts her statement that Agnes Mylles was guilty at the behest of Dorothy Baynton.

Henry and Dorothy also claim that Jane Marshall only gave evidence, accusing Dorothy of enticing Agnes, after receiving a corrupt payment by the plaintiffs. Jane agreed to retract her evidence as she was 'seeking more her liberty than to stand to the truth of the sayings and depositions therein by her before made'. In other words, she would do anything to be released from prison.

Jane Marshall in her answer in this case repeats that she thinks the murder was committed by Agnes Mylles and that it was by the procurement and enticement of Dorothy Baynton. She agrees that she was imprisoned in Salisbury and examined by the bailiff of Sarum and that whilst in prison she denied that the murder was done by Agnes Mylles. But she points out that she denied this only for fear of remaining in prison where she had been for half a year, and for fear of the 'continual urgent and fearful menaces and threats of the bailiff of Sarum and other Dorothy's friends who menaced and threatened her either to rot in prison and to lose her life'. Thus, Jane is really saying that she stands by her original statement that Agnes Mylles committed the murder at the request of Dorothy Baynton.

This case is characteristic of a particular type that were brought to the courts of equity: ones where perjury is suspected. If a case has already been heard in another court and has not gone the way the plaintiff hoped, it can be re-heard in the courts of equity on the grounds that the evidence which helped swing the case against the plaintiff was given under duress, or even worse under blackmail or bribery. This qualifies it to be heard in a court of equity, and so gains the plaintiff another chance to put their case.

Chapter 3

THE RECORDS

The records of the various different equity courts look similar and can be handled and interpreted in a similar way.

WHAT RECORDS LOOK LIKE PHYSICALLY

The physical appearance of Bills and Answers can be intimidating. They are large documents, and by the late seventeenth century can often measure over a metre in both directions. In some cases, particularly the nineteenth-century cases, they can be considerably bigger than this and can be up to 2m long. Before the late seventeenth century they are much more manageable. Some of the records are kept flat in boxes which makes them relatively easy to handle. Others, particularly the eighteenth- and nineteenth-century documents are quite unmanageable, with several bundles rolled together, and a researcher will need strength and lots of space to handle them. The documents are individually numbered, although it can be difficult to find the number as this is sometimes written on the front and sometimes on the back of the document.

The Bills and Answers require considerable concentration as not only are they physically large, but they can be fairly repetitive and so care needs to be taken not to slip a line. Generally the Bills and Answers, where they have the same reference, will be sewn together at the top left-hand corner, with the Bill on top and the Answer behind. However they can have become separated and now be listed with different reference numbers.

Interrogatories and Depositions have a very different appearance to the Bills and Answers in that they are usually much more

A typical Bill of Complaint, C 3/207/57.

manageable physically. The Town Depositions and Chancery or Country Depositions in the Court of Chancery are very different to look at. The Town Depositions are usually in good condition and laid flat in boxes, but it can be difficult to identify the correct one. Although of quite modest size, some of the Country Depositions are rather tightly bound and opening the roll can be awkward, though not as awkward as rolling them back up again as they spring open never to be returned to their original state.

Most of the other records, such as the Affidavits, Petitions, and Masters' Reports, are small and easily handled, however you need to be a weight-lifter to get the books of Orders and Decrees on to your table! The Exhibits are so varied in content and size that opening a box of mixed records is exciting but not very challenging physically, except perhaps for deeds which are usually of a reasonable size.

WHAT LANGUAGE ARE RECORDS WRITTEN IN AND HOW DIFFICULT IS THE PALAEOGRAPHY?

Unlike the courts of common law, the records of the courts of equity are all in English, except some of the very early medieval ones, which can be in Latin or Norman French.

Despite the physical difficulty of looking at pleadings, a bonus is that the handwriting is usually clear and consistent, although, as with all archives, time has taken its toll on some of them and they can be faded, stained, torn and otherwise difficult to read. The style of handwriting tends to be the same as that used in the wills of the Prerogative Court of Canterbury, so familiarity with this source should mean that there is no difficulty reading equity court Pleadings.

The handwriting in Depositions can be more difficult than that of the Bills and Answers, as they are often written hurriedly by a local clerk, rather than one of the Chancery clerks, however it is usually no more difficult than that of a locally proved will. As with the Pleadings, time has taken its toll on some of the documents and they have become faded or stained.

The handwriting of the Orders and Decrees is usually straightforward, however the abbreviations that are used can present difficulties until you are familiar with the records.

A DETAILED LOOK AT THE DOCUMENTS

This detailed look at the documents will give more idea of the sort of information that can be included and more particularly the sort of wording that is used. These descriptions are valid for all the courts of equity, although many of the types of document are now found only in the Court of Chancery

Pleadings: Bills and Answers

Bills of Complaint are easily identifiable as they start with such words, written in a large hand right across the top of the document as:

To the Right Honourable John Lord Eldon Baron Eldon of Eldon
in the county of Durham Lord High Chancellor of Great Britain

The document then usually starts with the 'Humbly complaining
unto your Lordship your orator . . .'. The name of the plaintiff is then
given. It is worth remembering at this point that the plaintiff is
known as the orator (or oratrix for a woman) throughout the Bill, as
the complainant throughout the Answer, and as the plaintiff in the
other documents.

There can be many plaintiffs and defendants, such as in the case
Slaney v Crump of 1721:[1]

Plaintiffs: John Slaney, baker (only son and heir and a
   residuary legatee of John Slaney, gent. late of Staplehurst,
   Kent and Elizabeth Slaney his wife, both deceased)
John Boyle, clothier of Cranbrooke, Kent and Elizabeth
   Boyle his wife
Lydia Troward (widow of Luke Troward, deceased)
Stephen Beesley of Christ Church, London and Sarah
   Beesley his wife
Thomas Maynard, clothier of Marden, Kent and Hannah
   Maynard his wife.
The said Elizabeth Boyce, Lydia Troward, Sarah Beesley and
   Hannah Maynard are daughters and residuary legatees of
   said John Slaney and Elizabeth Slaney.

Defendants: James Crump (brother in law of John Slaney)
Edward Deer alias Edmund Deer
William Lindfield
Daniel Austen and Mary Austen his wife (Mary is another
   daughter of John and Elizabeth Slaney).

The date of a Bill of Complaint can be difficult to find but is
usually somewhere at the top of the document, most commonly at
the top left corner.

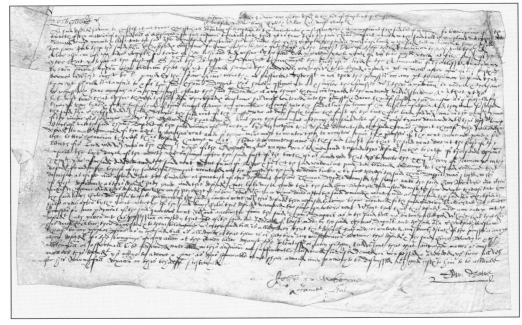

A typical Answer, C 3/207/57.

The names of the defendants will be found in the last two or three lines of a Bill of Complaint. The key phrase to look for is 'may it please your Lordship to grant unto your orator his Majesty's most gracious writ of subpoena to be directed to . . .' . This is then followed by the names of the defendants.

Answers start with such words, written in a large hand right across the top of the document as:

The joint and several answer of John Morgan and John Baker
to the Bill of Complaint of Theodosia Eyre Blosset an Infant by
her next friend complainant.[2]

The date of an answer is most often to be found in the bottom left corner, often with the place where it was sworn, but this is by no means always true, and it can also often be found at the top of the document.

A Bill of Complaint in the Duchy of Lancaster equity court will have slightly different opening words:

To the Right Honourable Sir Thomas Kirkby knight and baronet Chancellor of the Duchy of Lancaster.[3]

As might be expected, the opening words of a Bill of Complaint in the court of equity of the Palatinate of Lancaster are different again:

To the Right Honourable Sir John Otway knight Vice Chancellor of the County Palatine of Lancaster.[4]

The records for this court have rather different appearance as, although they are still fairly large and on parchment, they are folded and bound into volumes, in numerical order, which makes finding the correct one rather easier than trying to do the same in a box or a roll.

The Bills and Answers of the Palatinate of Durham are very similar to those of the other courts of equity, being rolled and boxed. The wording at the opening is of course different to allow for their being addressed to the Chancellor of the County Palatine of Durham and Sedbergh.

The Bills and Answers for the Exchequer court of the Palatine of Chester are in two series: the records in the first series (CHES 15) look very similar to those of the other equity courts, but those in the second series (CHES 16) are very different, being written on manageable-sized pieces of paper. Those in this second series tend to be for cases that concern money, loans and debts, rather than land. Cases concerning land are predominantly in the first series. The wording, however, is very similar to the records of the other equity courts. Both series contain documents other than Pleadings, such as Depositions. The Bills are addressed to the Chamberlain of the County Palatine of Chester.

Interrogatories and Depositions
The Interrogatories are the questions that will be put to the various deponents (witnesses) and will start with a phrase such as:

Interrogatories to be administered to witnesses to be produced, sworn and examined on the Part and behalf of John

Slaney, John Boyce and Elizabeth his wife, Lydia Troward widow, Stephen Beesley and Sarah his wife, Thomas Maynard and Hannah his wife in a Cause depending in the High Court of Chancery wherein they are complainants against James Crump, defendant.[5]

The individual questions are then listed and numbered, with the first question nearly always asking how long the deponent has known each of the parties, and any other person who is crucial to the case. In some cases the Interrogatories for both the plaintiff and defendant have survived, in some cases just one or the other.

The Depositions usually start with details of where they are taken, such as 'Depositions of witnesses taken at the house of Thomas Morthwaite innkeeper known by the sign of the White Swan in Clitheroe in the county of Lancaster the 14th day of January 1751'.[6] The Deposition of each deponent then starts with his/her name, age and occupation. The answers to the questions are then given in order and are numbered often with the word **Item** written in bold at the start of the answer to each new question. Each deponent will only answer the questions that are relevant to him/her.

The Depositions of the Palatinate of Lancaster are similar to those of the other courts in that fairly ordinary people made statements, such as those of a case between William Gaskell v Alexander Chorley gent, Edward Woods Alice Heys and George Taylor of 1692, heard at the house of Lawrence Gaskell of Rainford Co. Lancaster innkeeper:[7]

John Birchall of Rainford, Co. Lancs yeoman, age 60 years.
John Seddon of Sutton, Co. Lancs, butcher, age 34 years.
John Naylor of Hardshaw within Windle, Co. Lancs, yeoman, age 55 years.
Edward Rainford of Rainford, Co. Lancs, innkeeper, age 48 years.
James Penington of Upholland, Co. Lancs, yeoman, age 37 years.
Edmund Sephton of Rainford, Co. Lancs, yeoman, age 35 years.

A typical Deposition, STAC 3/80/1.

The signatures of the deponents in most cases, in all the equity courts, are an added bonus.

These records are tightly rolled and wrapped in boxes. The Depositions of the Palatinate of Durham are rolled individually with the Interrogatories and Depositions together, and then placed in a box.

Decrees and Orders

The Decrees and Orders are usually in large volumes, sometimes very, very large and heavy volumes, however where there are calendars, as with the Court of Chancery, the reference to the page number can be quite a relief as the correct entry can be found quickly although the handwriting in these can often be quite small and difficult to read. Many of the entries are purely administrative, such as requesting a defendant to put in his answer. Many, however, are much more interesting and can include a summary of the case, with details of other Orders, Petitions, Affidavits and Masters' Reports.

A typical Order will start with the words:

Upon motion this day made unto the court by xxx it was alleged . . .

Followed midway through with:

it was prayed that . . .

And ending with:

it was ordered that . . .

The later records are particularly rewarding as they also include references to all the documents that have been examined prior to the Order being made, such as indentures, parish registers, etc. In a very long and drawn-out case this Order of 1847 includes:[8]

And counsel for the petitioners upon hearing of the said petition, the probate of the will of Jane Bennett deceased the testatrix in the petition named, an order dated 24th August 1841, the Master's Report dated 11th July 1842, an order dated 26th July 1842, an indenture of assignment of 14th October 1839, and indenture dated 13th April 1842, an affidavit of John Smith verifying the due execution of the said indenture dated 14th October 1839 by Richard Russell Smith and Mary his wife parties thereto, an affidavit of Henry Workman verifying the execution of the said indenture dated 13th April 1842 by Richard Gibbs and Ann his wife and Mary Smith parties thereto, an extract from the Register of Burials of Weston Subedge in the county of Gloucester whereby it appears that Richard Russell Smith was buried on the 12th July 1840, and joint and several affidavit of John Tombs and Henry Workman verifying the said extract and identifying the said Richard Russell Smith as a party to the Deed of Assignment dated

14th October 1839, an extract from the Register of Marriages in the parish of Cheltenham in the county of Gloucester whereby it appears that George Hodgkins and Mary Smith were intermarried the 23rd December 1844, a joint and several affidavit of John Tombs and John Smith verifying the said extract and identifying the said Mary Smith as the widow of Richard Russell Smith, an extract from the Register of Burials in the parish of Offenham in the county of Worcester whereby it appears that Ann Gibbs was buried the 24th day of October 1846, a joint and several affidavit of Joseph Cole and Henry Workman verifying the said extract and identifying the said Ann Gibbs as the wife of Richard Gibbs named in the order made in this court dated 26th July 1842, and the Accountant General's certificate read, and what was alleged by the counsel for the petitioners.

A typical volume of Orders and Decrees.

No Orders and Decrees survive for the Court of the Star Chamber. Their loss was announced in 1719 by a Committee of the House of Lords which naively reported that 'they were last seen in a house in Bartholomew Close London'.

A volume of Orders and Decrees in the Duchy of Lancaster, the Palatinate of Durham or the Palatinate of Chester looks very similar to that of the Court of Chancery, but the handwriting is, if anything, rather clearer and there are more of the useful informative entries rather than purely administrative entries. The volumes can be very large and cumbersome, but the information included within makes any weightlifting that is required well worth the effort.

The means of reference to the Court of Chancery Orders and Decrees is via the calendars on the open shelves. These are divided into A and B books. Up to 1628 there is an A and a B book for each year, with identical information although usually one copy is in better condition. After 1629 the A and B refers to the part of the alphabet. All records from letter A to L are listed in the A books, and records from letter M to Z are listed in the B book.

When searching the calendars of Orders and Decrees it is worth remembering that the indexing can be slightly odd, such as titled people, who are notoriously difficult to find in an index. As an example, in a 1654 calendar all the entries for Lord X and Lady Y are under the letter L, including 'Lord Protector of the Commonwealth of England Scotland and Ireland'.

Before 1575 the calendars to the Orders and Decrees for the Court of Chancery are not on the open shelves and need to be ordered. The opening page of the calendar for 1576 is full of doodles by the clerks including 'Edwards is a knave'. Followed lower down the page by 'Edwardes is no knave, no more is Leonard Bantryn / Believe me thowe arte wise fellows. Jhon.' Even the calendars have a human touch!

Chancery Masters' Reports
These are the original reports made to the court by the Masters in Chancery. There are only a few before 1600, but from 1605 there are significant numbers.

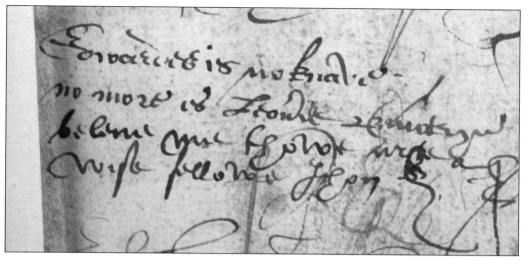

Doodling in a calendar of Orders and Decrees, IND 1/1432.

A short Master's Report might just be an allocation of costs relating to the case, but they can often be the most useful of all the documents relating to a case, in that they can summarise the Pleadings, they can recite the Interrogatories and Depositions, they can recite the Orders, include accounts and refer to the costs of the case.

The reports start with the words:

in pursuance of an order/decree . . .

A case is usually referred to a Master when there is factual evidence to be ascertained, such as the full accounts for a probate case or a mortgage case, the indentures for a marriage settlement case, the bonds for a case about debt, etc.

A Master's Report will usually end with words such as:

all which I humbly certify and submit to the grave judgement of this honourable court

Some of the Masters' Reports are very long (eighty-three pages in one nineteenth-century case) but most are rather shorter such as the one of 1698 relating to the case between Cuthbert Routh and

1 Junij 1698

Inter Jacob: Seamer Quer[entem]
Johem Johnson mil[item] Def[endentem]

In pursuance of an Ord[er] of the 5th day of March
last I have beene attended by the pl[aintif]s and defendant
and their Counsell and Solicit[or]s and considered of the
matters to mee referred And the pl[aintif]ts Counsell
before mee insisted that the defendant S[i]r John
Johnsons 1.2.3.4.5. and 6th Interrogatories and alsoe
his 16th and latter part of his 17th and the 21 Interri[es]
are Scandalous or impertinent and that the 29th
Interrogatory is leading And that the depositions
of Mary Powell Thomas Eakins Susannah Bury
Elizabeth Gibbs George Taylor Nowell Glover John
Randall Edmund Nicholson Richard Bromhole
Mary Graves Jonathan Bookey and ffrancis
Clark to the 6th Interrogatory And the depositions
of S[i]r Robert Bedingfeild to the 5th and 35 Interrogatir[ies]
and the depositions of Thomas Johnson to the 21
Interrogatory and of George Taylor to the 34th
Interrogatory are Scandalous or impertinent Upon
perusall and consideracon of which Interrogatoryes
and depositions I doe not find any matter of Scandall
therein And the defendant Johnson haveing by
his Answeare set forth seberall particular matters
in avoydance of matters charged or suggested by the
pl[aintif]ts Bill whereon the above mentioned Interrogatoryes
and depositions are founded And the pl[aintif]t haveing
replyed to the said Answeare I doe conceive the
said Interrogatoryes and depositions as this Case is
to be pertinent And upon perusall of the said
29th Interrogatory I doe conceive part thereof to be
leading (viz[t]) did the other and when declare or owne
that he had agreed or promised he would be content with a[l]
quarter part in the profitts of the said Trade In case the
said Marryage should take or had taken Effect All which
I humbly certifye and submitt to the grave Judgment
of this Hon[ora]ble Court.

Ric Holford .

A typical Master's Report, Seamer v Johnson, C 38/262.

Cuthbert Garth, his next friend, against Robert Lympson and his wife Elizabeth then called Eliza Routh, widow concerning a mortgage:[9]

> In pursuance of an order of the twenty eighty day of June one thousand six hundred ninety five I have in the presence of the plaintiffs' clerk in court and defendants solicitor allowed of a deed or indenture tripartite bearing even date with my report made between Richard Darnelly of Stanmore Magna in the county of Middlesex doctor of physic of the first part William Dixon of Clement Inn in the said county gent Receiver of the plaintiff's estate of the second part and the defendant Robert Lymson and Elizabeth his wife and the said Cuthbert Garth the plaintiffs next friend of the third part being a mortgage of certain messuages lands and tenements in Tottingham alias Tottenham in the said county of Middlesex in trust for the benefit of the plaintiff for the term of one thousand years for securing one hundred and sixty pounds raised and received by the said William Dixon out of the plaintiff's estate with interest for the same and paid by the said Wm Dixon to the said Richard Darnelly as in the said deed is mentioned which said deed I have approved of and do appoint the same to be executed by all the parties thereto named
>
> All which I humbly certify and submit to the grave judgement of this Honourable Court.
> Wm Cooke

A typical case where the Interrogatories and Depositions are questioned is also dated 1698, in the case between James Seamer plaintiff and John Johnson defendant.[10]

> In pursuance of an order of the 5th day of March last I have been attended by the plaintiff and defendant and their counsel and solicitors and considered of the matters to me referred.
>
> And the plaintiff's counsel before me insisted that the

defendant Sir John Johnson's 1, 2, 3, 4, 5, and 6th interrogatories and also the 16th and later part of the 17th and 21st interrogatories are scandalous or impertinent and that the 29th interrogatory is misleading.

And that the depositions of Mary Powell Thomas Hawkins Susannah Lucy Elizabeth Gibbs George Taylor Nowell Glover John Randall Edmund Nicholson Richard Bromhall Mary Graves Jonathan Bookey and Francis Clark to the 6th interrogatory, and the depositions of Sir Robert Bedingfield to the 5th and 35th interrogatories and the depositions of Thomas Johnson to the 21st interrogatory and of George Taylor to the 34th interrogatory are scandalous or impertinent. Upon perusal and consideration of which interrogatories and depositions I do not find any matter of scandal therein.

And the defendant Johnson having by his answer set forth several particular matters in avoidance of matters charged or suggested by the plaintiff's bill whereon the above mentioned interrogatories and depositions are founded.

And the plaintiff having replied to the said Answer I do conceive the said interrogatories and depositions for this case is to be pertinent.

And upon perusal of the said 29th interrogatory I do conceive part thereof to be leading (viz:) did he ever and when declare or own that he had agreed or promised he would be content with a quarter part in the profits of the said trade in case the said marriage should take or had taken effect.

All which I humbly certify and submit to the grave judgement of this honourable court.

A volume of reports in 1604 and 1605 is particularly rich in variety of subject and fascinating reading.[11] In the case between John Cotes and others v Jane Cotes alias Webster, the Master is not pleased at the credit of gentleman being blemished:

By virtue of an order of this honourable court dated 20 November 2 James I have considered the examination of the plaintiff John

Cotes touching the contempt thereby committed and do find first that he has in his said examination far strayed from the questions or interrogatories to him administered by large dilating upon collateral inducements of his sundry supposed excuses.

Next that he has thereby much touched and blemished the credit of a gentleman to whose trust and confidence this honourable court had formerly committed by their consents the indifferent hearing of their large and tedious suits, which in this time is usual though unworthy reward given unto all committed for their travel and pains

Lastly that he has not in my judgement by all his said discourses discharged or cleared himself of the said contempt.

As with all Chancery cases, the variety of subjects is almost limitless and another report in this volume concerns broken or merchantable glasses:

According to an order of 25th June last we have sundry times convened the parties before us and heard their mutual allegations and proofs concerning allowances for broken glasses amounting to £236 demanded by the defendant thus. By Articles of Agreement reduced into an indenture dated 8th April 40 Elizabeth it was covenanted among other things between the plaintiff and Mary one of the defendants during her widowhood that she should receive so many merchantable glasses during the space of two years of the plaintiff as she should weekly every Saturday pay £25 for and that the plaintiff should make her allowance of £130 for the first year and £100 the second year for such glasses as might be casually broken in the keeping and selling the same.

The defendant Michael not long after married the other defendant Mary and having continued the receiving of glasses and payment for the same according to the Articles of Agreement three quarters of the first year then ceased to

1691 June 21 Then Rec'd from John Anderton for 5
Store measures of Oats sold the Taylor of Cuper[?]   05 : 00 : 00

22. Rec'd of Dav'd Bagley y'[e] residue for y'[e] beasts sold 00 : 03 : 06

Rec'd from John peek's for 20 measures of
ffrench and Barley ————   01 : 13 : 4

26. Rec'd from Elizabeth Rowland for Rent 06 : 00 : 0

July   Rec'd from m'r Bent for 100 measures of Barley 12 : 10 : 00

Then Rec'd for 5 Store measures of Oats
of Thomas Taylor at 1'[s] p'[er] measure ———   05 : 00 : 00

3   Rec'd of John Greens for 40 measures
of Beanes and pease at 2'[s] 2'[d] p'[er] measure   04 : 06 : 0

23.   Rec'd of Eliz: Rawland for Rent —— 06 : 00 : 0

30.   Rec'd from marbury Bayliffes for
Gropenhall Lath ford Rents due mids last   09 : 01 : 0½

Sept. 4.   Rec'd of Hugh Worrall for the 100
measures of Barley sold him ——   03 : 00 : 00

Rec'd of Richard Gaudy for a Market Cart 00 : 10 : 00

Rec'd from him for a horse hide ——   01 : 00 : 00

Rec'd then at Weaverham for Lay of
Cattle in Weaverham Wood ——   12 : 17 : 04

Rec'd from John Anderton in p't of the
Lay of Beasts in Cogshall Lands belonging   10 : 09 : 6
to marbury this years ——

Oct. 9.   Rec'd of m'r Humphreys for one halfe y'[e]
Rent of one Close called Oxmore due Sep. 29 1691   03 : 15 : 0

Rec'd more for Lay of Cattle in Weaverham Wood 11 : 00 : 0

Rec'd from part of Weaverham Tenants
their Rents and Arrearages ——   10 : 19 : 2

Rec'd more for Lay of Beasts in Weaverham Wood 03 : 14 : 0

Rec'd then for Rent and arrearages of
Weaverham Tenants ——   02 : 03 : 7

Rec'd from Eliz: Rawland for Rent — 07 : 00 : 0

Rec'd from Richard Wrench a Bill of — 40 : 00 : 0

29   Rec'd from W'm Clough his Rent & Arrears 00 : 11 : 2

Nov. 30.   Rec'd for Lay of Beasts in Weaverham
Wood & some Rents and arrearages ——   02 : 15 : 6

4   Rec'd from Eliz: Rawland more Rent — 21 : 00 : 0

12   Rec'd from Edward Basnett for Lay
of a Colt at marbury ——   00 : 12 : 00

Rec'd of Thomas Taylor for Oats by
Richard Massy ——   03 : 00 : 00

receive any more or to make payment for the same, rather through the default of the defendants than of the plaintiff as we conceive upon the proof produced before us which proof stood upon and witness and some other strong presumptions afterward Appesley the defendant puts the covenant of allowance for broken glasses in suit for the whole two years and recovers by judgment £280 odd pounds.

How far the plaintiff is now to be relieve in this court upon the privity of this matter we humbly leave to your Lordship's decision.

The case between Bewes v Green and others in this same volume gives the Master's opinion on Cornishmen:

I have as I was by order of this court appointed considered of the plaintiffs and of the answers of the four defendants thereto whereby I find the old imputation laid upon my countrymen to be true, that Cornishmen will go to law for the waging of a straw, for here in this bill the plaintiff being a Cornishman served 4 of his neighbours for that he having driven an end betwixt one of the defendants and another for 30s in a suit depending betwixt them upon an action of the case in the Kings Bench wherein he was provised to be saved harmless for that the attorneys in that court took fees of 10s apiece for the suit there depending there was recovered by one of the defendants £3 3s 4d of the plaintiff by action whereupon he did put the other in suit for whom he had compounded in which suit he was overthrown and to give colour to this wrongful suit he alleges that he delivered to one of the plaintiff's wives certain evidences to be kept by her who combining with the other 3 defendants two of his neighbours and their wives parties to this bill affirm that he has no witnesses either of the promise made to him for the saving of him harmless or of the delivery of the deeds which being expressly denied by the defendants in their answers for that this suit appears to be raised only for vexation I think it fit that the defendants should be dismissed and to have £4 for their costs of the plaintiff which I might well have doubled it if had not been for country sake.

The Masters' Reports are full of phrases that epitomise the spirit of the equity courts such as:

meet that the injunction should be granted for the stay of the defendants suit at the common law according to the petition of the plaintiff . . .

And I think it fit that the defendants should answer that point . . .

But it falls out somewhat questionable in conscience whether the defendants ought to pay the half years rent payable to the Lord Morley at Michaelmas 1602 . . .

I had the parties before me, the plaintiff himself with his solicitor appearing and the defendant's brother for her, betwixt whom although I sought to have set some quiet and yet I found not their inclinations bent to accept of any . . .

Chancery Masters' Exhibits

This class of documents is one of the richest in the whole series. The variety here is perhaps even greater than in the Masters' Reports and the Pleadings. The Exhibits are the documents that have been used during the case as evidence, and instead of being returned to their owner at the end of the case, have remained with the court.

Deeds and accounts are probably the most common documents to remain as Exhibits. Some of these are well catalogued, others are only found as a result of lucky dip.

A case dated 1768 titled Blythe v Chapman includes a vast number of deeds concerning lands in Northampton, in a box of Exhibits dating from 1625 such as:[12]

1st Dec 1713
Lease to Moses Walton of House and Lands in Ravensthorp
   from Mich 1713 at the Rent of 33d per annum
Indenture between:
William Chapman of Bethnal Green, Middlesex, gentleman of
   the first part
Moses Walton of Ravensthorpe in Northampton, yeoman of
   the other part.

22 June 1742
Indenture of three parts (Edward Chapman, James Lowther,
Geff Wall);
Edward Chapman of the City of London, linendraper Son and
heir of William Chapman formerly of the City of London,
clerk, and late of the Hamlet of Bethnal Green in the Parish of
Stepney Middlesex Minister of the Gospel deceased by the
Anne Chapman one of the Daughters of Edward Lewis late of
London sugar refiner his late wife since also deceased
James Lowther of Warwick Lane London, gentleman
Jeffry Wall of Saffron Walden in Essex, gentleman of the third
part.

19th May 1701 13th William III.
Indenture Tripartite between
Thomas Chapman of the City of Coventry
William Chapman of the city of London
Joseph Olds of the City of Coventry and Thomas Lander of
   Allesley in the county of Warwick Gent
Lease and Release.

31st July 1704
Moses Walton's Lease and Bond for Nine Years.
Between:
William Chapman of the Parish of Stepney in County
   Middlesex, gentleman

Moses Walton of Ravensthorpe Northants, husbandman of
the other part.
Grants Ground Lott and Farm Lott to Moses Walton
This Lease expires at Lady Day 1714.

21st June 1742
Indenture between:
Edward Chapman London, Linendraper, Eldest son and heir
of William Chapman, formerly of City of London, Clerk and
late of Hamlet Bethnall Green Parish of Stepney, Middlesex,
Minister of the Gospell deceased by Ann Chapmen one of the
daughters of Edward Lewis late of London Sugar refiner his
late wife since also deceased
James Lowther of Warwick Lane London, gentleman
Jeffry Wall of Saffron Walden in Essex, gentleman of the third
part.

The catalogue for these documents merely reads 'Title deeds relating
to Ravensthorpe, Northants'. Other cases are rather better described
in the online catalogue, such as the documents relating to Moore v
Daniel which include:[13]

Deeds and indentures of fines relating to Dublin and Wicklow, Ireland.	1675
Deeds and indentures of fines relating to Tyrone, Ireland.	1676
Deeds, bills, accounts etc of the Earl and Countess of Drogheda.	1677–1704
Orders, depositions etc in various chancery suits.	1679–1708
Commissions in a regiment of Foot Guards.	1680, 1681
Memorandum book of William Moore, containing accounts, recipes, cures etc.	1674–1685
Deeds and indentures of fines relating to Down, Ireland.	1682
Extracts from will of William Moore.	1682

Correspondence and accounts of the dowager	1684–1697
Countess of Meath, wife to William Moore.	1692
Will of Dacres Barrett.	
Deeds and indentures of fines relating to London,	1697
Surrey, Kent, Essex and Herts.	
Extract of testament dative of William, Earl of	1704
Dalhousie.	
Copy of will of Anne, countess of Sunderland, and	1712
executor's papers: Northants.	
Will of William Moore: Dublin and Co Monaghan,	1714
Ireland.	
Deeds and indentures of fines relating to Tipperary,	1722
Ireland.	
Letters to William Moore from Jean Serres, a	1725–1727
French Protestant who had spent 28 years in	
the galleys.	

It will be noted that many of these documents relate to Ireland. A closer look at some of them shows the detail of the place names involved, such as:

Indenture Quinque Partite, 2nd August 1722
The town of Fethard, the farm of Killock, the town and lands of Coolemore and Coolemure, the towns and lands of Dromdeele Currareagh and Corbally, the towns and lands of Bannackstown and Ballyknockane, all which are lying and situated in the Barony of Middlethird in the county of Tipperary.

and

Indenture, 1st June 1682
Dufferin, Killyleagh, Bangor, Holliwood, Ballywalter, Armillin, Newcumber and Balleportavo also Portavo, Ballemulleragh also Groomsport, and many others, all in county Down.

95

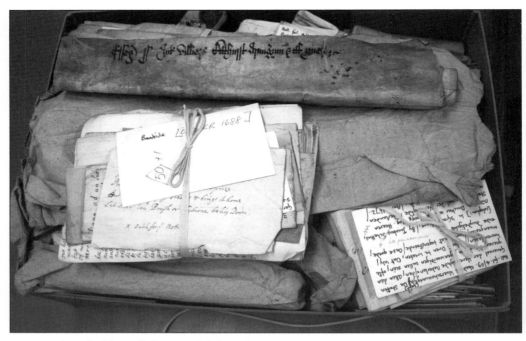

A typical box of Masters' Exhibits, C 110/80.

This particular box of Exhibits also contains many items relating to lands held in London:

> Indenture, 30th September 1686
> Between Thomas Vitcher citizen and fishmonger of London on the one part and the Honourable William Moore Esq of Mellifort in the Kingdom of Ireland of the other part.
> King Square alias Frith Square, Parish of St Martin in the Fields and St Giles in the Fields, London.

The Exhibits alone can tell a typical equity court story, of general human failing and feuding.

A case of 1816 is simply described as 'Deeds and papers relating to Ridley's bankruptcy and the sale of his property: Tenbury, Worcs'.[14] This box reveals property plans, deeds and many other documents of interest to a local historian, particularly of the Hop Pole Inn in Tenbury:

Life and fire insurance documents

The Hop-Pole Inn, Tenbury; a Capital Inn, freehold dwelling houses and premises in Tenbury in Worcester, and a freehold estate in the Parish of Caynham in the County of Salop which is to be Sold by Auction.

Auction certificate

Conditions of sale

Particulars of sale. with details such as 'A very neat and desirable new-erected DWELLING-HOUSE, Sash Front, Brick-built and Tiled, situate on the east side of Team-street' (LOT 1.)

LOT 2. HOP-POLE INN – 'very substantial and spacious DWELLING-HOUSE, with elegant Sash Front, containing an Entrance and two very large Parlours in front, well fitted up, painted and papered in the modern taste, each 16 feet by 13 feet, spacious Bar, 16 feet by 9 feet'

LOTS 5, 6 and 7 are seat/pew/kneelings in the Parish Church of Tenbury.

Ground/floor plan for the site

Biddings for the Hop-pole Inn

Warrant of seizure

Dividends

Bargain and Sale of the Real Estate of George Ridley a Bankrupt; Provisional Assignment of the Estate and Effects of George Ridley a Bankrupt; Assignment of the Goods, Chattels &c of George Ridley a Bankrupt; Counterpart Assignment of the Goods, Chattels &c of George Ridley a Bankrupt.

Boxes of Exhibits can also include pedigrees, such as the case of Mapp v Ellcock of 1831 which includes a pedigree of Mrs Pare's family.[15] A more decorative pedigree relating to the Crispin family of Creacombe in Devon is found in a box of pedigrees from 'unknown causes'.[16]

On a completely different note, and to illustrate the wide variety of documents that are included in the Chancery Masters' Exhibits,

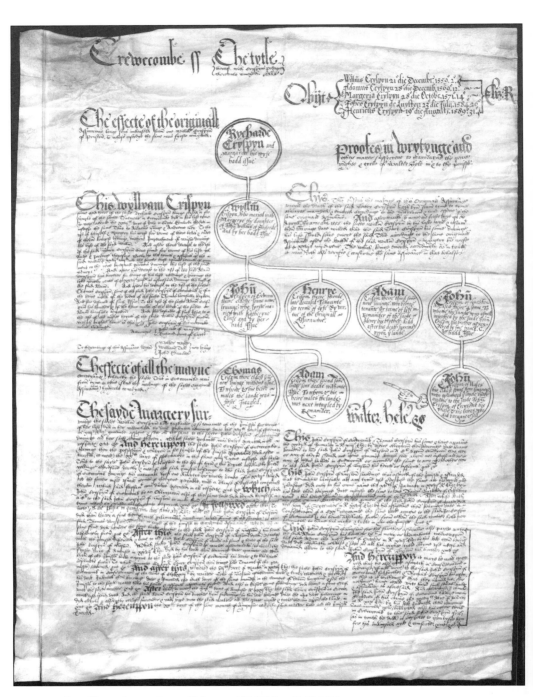

A pedigree from a box of Masters' Exhibits, C 103/18.

98

there are several documents relating to the ownership of slaves in America. In one case the catalogue entry simply reads: 'C 108/174 PARKINSON v INGRAM: Estates in Jamaica of John Parkinson of London, merchant. Accounts and lists, including a list of black slaves: Middx, Jamaica, WI, 1778–1794'.[17] In fact there is very much more to the box of documents. The case regards the sale of certain lands, plantations, slaves, cattle etc. by John Parkinson of Watling Street in the City of London to William Boats of Liverpool, Merchant, Francis Ingram Liverpool Merchant, John Kaye Liverpool Merchant, John Stabler of Watling Street Merchant and James Webster and David Webster both of the City of London Merchants. The cause of the sale is that John Parkinson is indebted to these people; a Schedule attached shows how much he owes to the individuals. John Parkinson possesses various estates, lands, plantations, etc. in Westmoreland, Jamaica, with much of it deriving from indentures and agreements between him and Martin Williams of Montego Bay in the Parish of Saint James, Jamaica. The lands include the Seven

Detail from a pedigree from a box of Masters' Exhibits, C 103/18.

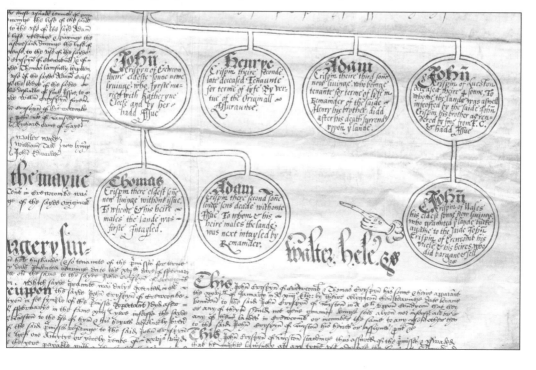

Rivers Estate in the parish of St James and Bickerstaff Penn Estate. Seven Rivers is a place that still exists today. From the historian's point of view, the most interesting part of the case is what is being sold along with the plantations: sugar works, rum, slave lists, cattle, etc. The slave lists are illuminating, whilst to modern eyes being quite shocking with reams of names listed next to their prices in the same Schedule as that where the cattle are listed. Most only have first names: 'Fortune', 'Daniel', 'Colin', some seem to be almost nicknames, 'Brave Boy', 'One leg Blackburry' 'Little Will', 'Old Blackwall', 'Black Dirk', 'Creole George'. Some of the names make us feel uncomfortable today, with references to their race. A good number of the names are very anglicised such as 'Tim', 'Bonny', 'Bob', 'Charles', 'Peter', 'Christmas', 'Margaret' and 'Sally'. The slaves are split into categories, and have different skills: 'field negro', 'working children' (particularly sad) and 'young children' (sadder!). Young children are mostly described in their family units. The papers show the jobs for the slaves and how many of each:

Drivers	5
Coopers	7
Carpenters	3
Wheelwrights	4
Masons	4
Sawyers	6
Head cattle and Mulemen	3
Field Men	93
Cattle boys	19
Field Women	124
Washers at Montego Bay	2
Children that work	29
Children about the G. house	5
Young children	83
Able negroid at Bickerstaff	38
Total:	434

Extract from a slave list in a box of Masters' Exhibits, C 108/174.

Other skilled jobs that are mentioned include smiths, gardeners, cartmen, watermen, distillers. The above names and figures refer to those on the Seven Rivers Estate; there is a similar list referring to Bickerstaff Penn Estate.

Another box of Exhibits of 1804 contains similar information.[18] This case is described in the catalogue as: 'Chambers v. Goldwin: Correspondence and papers of Abraham Henry Chambers with

101

James Shand in Jamaica concerning sugar plantations, slaves etc. on the estates of the late Mr Ratcliffe.' This box mainly consists of correspondence between Abraham Henry Chambers, London and James Shand, manager of his estates in Jamaica. It includes a valuation of both of his estates, Exeter Estate (valued at £43,474) and Greenwich Estate (valued at £54,299). The valuation of Exeter Estate includes: 'Cane Pieces & Corn Land'; 'Buildings, Works and Fixtures'; 'Stock viz'; 'Slaves' . This list of slaves gives each slave's 'name', 'occupation', 'condition' and 'country' and price. The column for 'condition' refers to being 'healthy' or 'lame', 'sickly', 'runaway', 'able', 'old', 'infirm', 'old and ruptured', 'weak', 'invalid', 'weakly', 'elephantiasis', 'a child'. Most of the slaves are 'Creole'.

We also see 'Eboe' (commonly known today as Igbo from the Bight of Biafra), 'Papaw' (Fon people from between Volta and Lagos on the Slave Coast), 'Coromantee' (peoples from the Gold Coast), 'Chamba' (from the Gold Coast hinterland), 'Congo', 'Nago' (a sub-group of the Yoruba people) and 'Succo'. Some of the slaves in these Schedules are noted as being 'runaways' or 'notorious runaways'. We also find Schedules enclosed, shipping documents and lists of medical supplies.

The letters enclosed in this Exhibit give us an insight into the private feelings of John Shand, and almost have a diary feel. The personal tone and inflection of the letters really bring them to life. They inform us not only of the opinions of white planters, but also the historical and social context, and an insight into what it was like to farm in Jamaica, and his opinions on the slaves he worked with.

In these a desire is shown to not treat them inhumanely, however to our eyes lots of the words used in reference to them seem dehumanising in themselves:

At my last visit I served out to the negroes their annual allowance of cloth. It has been usual to impart for them a few piece of callimance, I believe they call the stuff for petticoats. This is pretended to be for breeding women but knowing that it is usually distributed to a few favourites who have heart rise for indulgence I struck my pen through it amongst other things in raising the last of supplies given in by the Overseer. In place of these, I allow on my own estates as much striped blue and white linseed as will make a petticoat for each woman. In distributing them I pay attention to the claims of mothers of children and to the miserable subjects who must be found on every plantation, who have nothing except what their master allows and sees, make up for them as for children who are incapable of taking care of themselves.

As I have before hinted to you the slaves on Exeter are very superior to those at Greenwich in moral habits, in physical strength and capability of improvement.

It gives me infinite satisfaction to find that your ideas of the treatment of the negroes coincide with my own. I am afraid that the comforts of the poor people on these plantations have been less attended to than would have been proper.

In addition to the necessary article of a little clothing the chief claim they make on their master is for Herrings. This is the principal ingredient in seasoning all their food and I think has been dealt out with too sparing a hand. To come to particulars the quantity received this year will serve thirty weeks at the rate to three Herrings weekly to each negro. For the remainder of the year they must go without this necessary corrective of their acescent diet or purchase it from their little peculium. The richer and more provident can find a supply, the poor and sickly cannot, the consequences are often as fatal to the interests as they are disgraceful to the humanity of the master.

There are also references to the farming which is generally represented as being difficult and unreliable. Letter, 2 July 1803:

We have in here been tantalised with appearances of rains and have just had enough to keep the canes alive and preserve our hopes that there may yet be a crop next year, but no regular season has fallen and we despair of having the earth fully saturated before October.

A drought as has happened this year after the time of writing for supplies may totally defeat what was then the reasonable expectation of a planter.

There are also references to the socio-political situation/context:

I had nothing in view but the good of the plantation; the same end renders it proper in me to observe that should the war continue there is great reason to believe that shipping may be scarce next year.

The first day of August is the regular date for the discharge of all claims on planters and consequently all other annual accounts.

Had I at an earlier period foreseen the recurrence of war, the rum of which about forty puncheons have been sent to market in Kingston should also have been shipped for London.

Provisions have, as might be expected, taken a great rise in the market of Kingston since hostilities commenced. Independent of the increased freight and charges we have already to feed a thousand prisoners of war. Speculators contemplate a considerable increase of that number and an augmentation of the naval and military force.

As the number of slaves is very little different and our present deficiency law will require an establishment of white people exactly similar to be kept up, the clothing, food and comforts proper for the one, will be requisite on the other. [The deficiency law was designed to retain a minimum number of whites on each plantation to safeguard against slave revolts.]

But every thing in Vere farming is uncertain and precarious to the last moment.

On well conducted estates it is the practice to sell the Rum in Kingston, whilst the sugars only are supplied to Great Britain.

Masters' Documents

At the time of writing these are in the process of being listed.

There is an index for each of the series of Masters, and these are then listed under the name of the last Master in each series. Preliminary work by TNA indicates that the nineteenth-century listing of these documents in the indexes are inaccurate, as about 20 per cent of the references seem to lead nowhere. A full list of the Chancery Masters is available in the paper catalogue introduction for C 103.

Cause Books

The Cause books for the Court of Chancery were used by the court to note the receipt of Pleadings from the late seventeenth century. They are difficult to use before 1842, however from 1842 they are written in tabular form, with alterations and additions throughout the period of the case, and can thus be a little difficult to interpret, in much the same way as the Estate Duty registers.

Affidavits

Many of the Affidavits concern the delivery of writs of subpoena by the clerks to the defendants and so are of marginal interest to historians, however a good number do contain useful information. Although there is a preponderance of Affidavits in London, there are also many for places elsewhere. There are series of both registers of Affidavits, and original Affidavits. The registers are useful as they include some Affidavits where the original has not survived. The original documents of course are interesting as they contain original signatures. The Affidavits are numbered so the original and registered copy can be matched. Generally the registers are easier to search as they are better indexed.

Looking at a sample volume for 1644 the following are found:[19]

No. 297
Peter Julian v Richard Hull
13th December 1644
Affidavit by Bartholomew Lurpeire of the parish of St Anne

Blackfriars London aged 31 years or thereabouts maketh oath that he well knoweth the complainant and knoweth Mrs Malvin in the bill named who hath confessed to this deponent that the rings in question are the goods of the complainant.

And she did receive them from him under pretence to show them to some lady

And that she wanting money did pawn them to the defendant Hull for £10 and no more whereupon the complainant and this deponent went to the house of the said defendant Hull and demanded the said rings of him and offered to pay him the £10 with the interest but the said Hull refused the same.

And the said complainant then told this deponent that he would commence suit against him for recovery of them and accordingly did which is the suit now depending.

And the said complainant being as a merchant and bound for Portugal left the managing of the suit to some friends.

And since he is arrived at Lisbon as by several letters from the said complainant may appear whereof one bearing date in July last wherein he does make mention of the business and of returning homeward either in September or October last so that he is daily expected.

This next one gives an insight into the reality of living during the Civil War, and the fear of being thought to support the 'wrong' side.

No. 308
William Turrell Esq. v Nicholas Southcott
8th January 1644
Whereas Robert Bickers of Widley co Southampton has seen and heard read a copy of an affidavit by the plaintiff in the court of Chancery purporting amongst other things that the said plaintiff enquired after the said defendant of one Bickers at whose house the said defendant usually lodged and had done for some time last past before the date of the said

affidavit and that the said Bickers informed the plaintiff that the said defendant was gone from his the said Bickers house and carried with him all his goods to the city of Winchester and that the said defendant was going to the King's army to serve therein against the Parliament and that the said defendant by reason of his malignant speeches and carried at this the said Bickers house and other places thereabouts has caused the said Bickers to be put to great trouble and to be imprisoned as a malignant as by the said affidavit purporting to be sworn 9th July 1644 more at large appears.

Now the said Robert Bickers makes oath that he conceives and believes that the said Bickers named in the affidavit is meant and intended to be him this deponent for true it is that the said plaintiff did before the making of the said affidavit enquire of this deponent after the said defendant and true it is that the said defendant did heretofore usually lodge at this deponents house at Widley aforesaid and that this deponent told the said plaintiff that the said defendant was gone from his house and carried with him a trunk or two of his and his sisters clothes to Winchester and that the said defendant did intend from thence to go into his native county in Devonshire, but his deponent denies absolutely that he at any time ever told the said plaintiff that the said defendant had carried away all his goods with him to Winchester or that he was gone to the King's army to serve therein against the parliament or that the said defendant by reason of his malignant speeches and carriage at this deponent's house and other places thereabouts had caused this deponent to be put to great or any trouble at all or to be imprisoned as a malignant, as is most unjustly and scandalously affirmed in the said affidavit.

And this deponent further makes oath that the said defendant did never in any wise to this deponent's knowledge or observation appear or show himself in any wise to be a malignant against the parliament nor ever told this deponent that he would go to the king to serve him against the

107

parliament but always carried himself when he was in this deponent's company, in a civil and well wishing way to the parliament.

And this deponent does verily believe that the affidavit was made more out of malice than otherwise and for the said plaintiff's own end and against the said defendant for that the said defendant has now a suit depending at law against the said plaintiff for a great sum of money which he owes to the said defendant by bond.

Signed: Robert Bickers

This next example is also from during the Civil War, but seems to show that many aspects of life continued as usual:

No. 3
8th May 1644
Robert Myller v Edmund Coker and others
Wm Horton makes oath upon Saturday 13th April last he went to the Queenes Armes near Holborn Bridge where he was credibly informed that that there had been two carriers with wagons which went from Salisbury to London that week. And that the one of them John Hylliard went from thence the same day the week then next following this deponent went to Gerrards hall near Bread street and to the King's Head in the old Change and to the said Queens Arms.

At all which places he was credibly informed that divers persons living in New Sarum in the county of Wiltshire were then in London and that at this present time there are divers citizens and inhabitants of Salisbury aforesaid in London which came lately from Salisbury and do usually pass to and fro without any let or interruption.

Signed: Ro: Riche

Looking at another random volume in 1727 we find similarly useful Affidavits:[20]

No. 623
22 May 1727
Philip Broke infant v Richard Norton an infant
Philip Bacon of Ipswich co Suffolk gent receiver appointed by
the High and Honourable Court of the rents and profits of the
complainant's estate in cause makes oath that he this
deponent was very well acquainted and lived in friendship
with Robert Broke the elder and Robert Broke the younger
Esq. the plaintiff's father and elder brother both since
deceased and likewise that he this deponent has known the
estate in question for the space of 28 years or thereabouts and
has had the care and management of it for some time passed
and also that he this deponent has already by the order and
direction of this Honourable Court laid out and disposed of in
the purchase of South Sea annuities for the benefit and
advantage of the plaintiff and his family the full sum of £2,000
being part of what he this deponent has received of the rents
and profits of the said estate and this deponent likewise says
that he this deponent has now in his hands custody or power
the full sum of £100 the other part of the produce of the said
estate to lay out and dispose of as this Honourable Court shall
direct and this deponent further says that admitting this High
and Honourable Court shall think fit to make an additional
allowance for the £100 remaining there will notwithstanding
be in this deponents hands custody or power together with
what is so laid out as aforesaid at or by the time of the
plaintiff's attaining the age of 21 years in as he this deponent
shall so long live, the full sum of £300 and upwards unforeseen
accidents excepted.

The records of the courts of equity can be helpful in unearthing
information about servants and how they see rather more of the
activities of their masters than was perhaps intended, as this
Affidavit shows:

No. 308
7 July 1727
Thomas Gunton v Laurence Paine
Tristram Brampfield of Bridgwater co Somerset gent and John Pittman of Bridgwater tailor do jointly make oath that some time in the month of March last past one Thos Lovibond who was at that time a domestic servant to the defendant Lawrence Paine informed this deponent that his master had often told him that he should never take notice of his wife (to wit the above named Elizabeth Paine) nor mind what she said for that she should not be mistress in his house as long as Mrs Harrison was there, that he said Thos Lovibond should always take the said Mrs Harrison for his mistress and obey her in all respects for he loved her better than his wife and the said Thos Lovibond further informed this deponent that the said Lawrence Paine did use Mrs Paine his wife very bad and always in an uncommon way and took more notice of Mrs Harrison than his wife and would very often see Mr Paine and the said Mrs Harrison very familiar together and the said Tristram Bampfield and the said John Pittman further make oath that they have often within a month past heard (one Mary Cife another domestic servant of the said Lawrence Paine) her to say that Mr Paine told her she should not mind his wife but Mrs Harrison.

Petitions

Petitions are some of the most useful documents. They are usually Petitions to the court by one of the parties, or by someone affected by the case, asking for something to be done by the court, such as money to be released. They often contain a good deal of background information concerning the case including new information that is not included in the main Bill and Answer, and always ends with a request to the court for a particular order.

They can include information such as that found in the case between Nicholas Donnithorne Esq., executor of Isaac Donnithorne, clerk, deceased who was executor of Elizabeth Donnithorne, spinster, deceased and the defendants Thomas Wallis, Robert Wallis and Jane Wallis, widow.[21] In this case the Petition is by the plaintiff and refers back to an earlier case:

> Showeth that the late plaintiff Elizabeth Donnithorne in or about Hilary Term 1774 exhibited her original bill of complaint against Martin Wallis since deceased thereby stating amongst other things that by indenture dated 16th November 1759 made between (1) John Trevennen clerk (2) the then defendant Martin Wallis and (3) the then plaintiff Elizabeth Donnithorne
>
> Reciting as in the said indenture is recited it is witnessed that in consideration of £801 paid by the said Elizabeth Donnithorne to said John Trevennen (the original mortgagee of the premises after mentioned) by the direction of the said Martin Wallis (the original mortgagor of the premises) and also of £29 to the said Martin Wallis paid also by the said Elizabeth Donnithorne the said John Trevennen by the direction of the said Martin Wallis did convey and the said Martin Wallis did confirm unto the said Elizabeth Donnithorne certain freehold premises situate in the parish of St Buryan in the county of Cornwall called Tredinney otherwise Terdinney otherwise Tredennye
>
> To hold to the said Elizabeth Donnithorn her heirs and assigns for ever subject to the proviso after mentioned
>
> And the said indenture further witnessed that for the considerations aforementioned the said John Trevennen by the like directive of the said Martin Wallis did ratify and confirm to the said Elizabeth Donnithorne a moiety of a certain leasehold tenement called Brane and several closes of leasehold land with the appurtenances in the said indenture particularly mentioned
>
> To hold the said Elizabeth Donnithorne her executors administrators and assigns from the death of one Mary Wallis for the term therein to come if the lives therein named should so long exist

111

With a proviso for redemption of all the said premises on payments by the said Martin Wallis his heirs executors administrators or assigns to the said Elizabeth Donnithorne her executors administrators or assigns of the sum of £830 with lawful interest for the same on the 15th November next

And the said Elizabeth Donnithorne prayed by her original bill that the said Martin Wallis might be decreed to pay her the said £830 and all interests due and to grow due for the same together with her costs, and in default thereof that the said Martin Wallis might be foreclosed from all equity of redemption in the said premises

That the said Elizabeth Donnithorne died on 17th April 1774 having first made her will and appointed the late plaintiff Isaac Donnithorne her executor and residuary legatee who in Michaelmas Vacation 1774 filed his Bill of Revivor in this honourable court against the said Martin Wallis and also against the said defendant Joseph Donnithorne the heir at law of the said plaintiff Elizabeth Donnithorne, thereby stating those matters and praying that the said suit might be revived against the said Martin Wallis and Joseph Donnithorne as therein mentioned

That afterwards, videlicet in April 1776 the said Martin Wallis died whereupon the then plaintiff Isaac Donnithorne exhibited his Bill of Revivor and Supplement against the defendants Robert Wallis, Thomas Wallis and Jane Wallis thereby stating that the said Martin Wallis made his will and devised his interest in the mortgaged premises to his sons the defendants Thomas Wallis and Robert Wallis their heirs and executors or administrators, it was therefore prayed that the said suit might be revived against the said defendants Robert Wallis Thomas Wallis and Jane Wallis

That the said defendant Thomas Wallis (who was the said Martin Wallis's heir at law) and the said defendant Robert Wallis (who was the said Martin Wallis's sole executor) by their several Answers to the said Bill of Revivor and Supplement filed on the death of the said Martin Walis admitted the Indenture of Mortgage dated 16th November 1759 and that the said £830 and all interest for the same was then due and that the late defendant Martin Wallis duly made and executed his will dated the 13th April 1776 whereby he gave and devised to the defendant Thomas Wallis (amongst other things) part of the said mortgaged freehold premises to hold to him and his heirs for ever, and the testator also gave to his son the defendant Robert Wallis all the rest of the said mortgaged freehold premises to hold to him and to his heirs for ever and the testator gave and bequeathed all the rest of his effects of what nature or kind soever unto his said son Robert Wallis whom he constituted sole executor of his said will, and the defendants Thomas Wallis and Robert Wallis claimed to be entitled to such share and interest in the said mortgaged premises was devised to them respectively by the said will subject to the said mortgage

That by the Decree made on the hearing of this Cause dated 22nd April 1782 it was ordered and decreed (amongst other things) that it should be referred to Mr Ord to take an Account of what was due to the then plaintiff Isaac Donnithorne as executor of the late plaintiff Elizabeth Donnithorne for principal and interest on the said mortgage and to tax the then plaintiff and the late plaintiff Elizabeth Donnithorne their costs of this suit and upon the defendant Thomas Wallis's paying unto the then plaintiff what should be found due to him for principal interest and costs as aforesaid within six months after the said Master should have made his Report it was ordered and decreed that the then plaintiff did (as standing in the place of the said late plaintiff Elizabeth Donnithorne) reconvey and reassign the said mortgaged premises free from all encumbrances and deliver up all deeds in his custody upon oath to the said defendant Thomas Wallis

But in default of the said defendant Thomas Wallis's paying

the same unto the then plaintiff as aforesaid the said Thomas Wallis was from thenceforth to stand foreclosed from all Equity of Redemption to the said Mortgaged Premises

That the said Decree has been passed and entered and since pronouncing the said decree the late plaintiff Isaac Donnithorne died having first made his will and appointed your petitioner executor thereof who has since duly proved the same and upon whose death videlicet in Michaelmas term 1782 the petitioner filed his bill of Revivor against all the said defendants who all appeared thereto and their time for answering any expired videlicet on 6th March 1783 the said suit and proceedings were by the order of this Honourable Court duly revived against the defendants

That in pursuance of the said Decree the petitioner proceeded before the said Master to take the accounts and tax the costs directed by the said Decree when upon preparing the Draft of the Master's Report your petitioner discovered and was advised that the said Decree ought to have directed, amongst other things, that upon the defendants Thomas Wallis's and Robert Wallis's paying the then plaintiff what should be reported due to him for principal interest and costs thereof the said Thomas Walis and Robert Wallis should from thenceforth stand foreclosed from all Equity of Redemption in the mortgaged premises the said Robert Wallis being not only entitled to a part of the said mortgaged freehold premises called Terdinney as devise thereof as aforesaid but also entitled to the said mortgaged leasehold premises as sole executor and residuary legatee of his said late father Martin Wallis the mortgagor

But the name of the said Robert Wallis was omitted in the said Decree by mistake in drawing up the same

Your petitioner therefore humbly prays your Lordship that the said Cause may be reheard and that the said Decree may be varied by ordering the defendant Robert Wallis as well as the defendant Thomas Wallis to pay your Petitioner what shall be reported due to him for principal interest and costs and in default thereof that both the said defendants Thomas Wallis and Robert Wallis may be absolutely foreclosed from all Equity of Redemption or that your Lordship will be pleased to make such other Order in the premises as to your Lordship shall seem meet.

Account Books

Not all the account books survive, but the Masters' Accounts for the period 1750–1850 have been described in the online catalogue. There are many references to accounts kept by the Accountant General relating to individual Chancery cases. From 1726 some records survive, however there is no easy means of access to them.

Key Phrases in Pleadings

The aim of this section of the book is to show the typical phrases that occur in the documents.

A Bill of Complaint starts with a phrase such as:

> Humbly Complaining unto your Lordship your Orators William Robinson the younger of Toynton St Peters near Spilsby in the County of Lincoln Farmer and Samuel Robinson of No. 12 Great Marlborough Street within the liberty of the City of Westminster in the County of Middlesex Gentleman.

Background information is then given such as:[22]

> That the said Joseph Robinson late of East Keal in the said County of Lincoln Farmer deceased your Orator's late Uncle and the Testator hereinafter named was in his lifetime and at the time of making his Will and of his death hereinafter mentioned seized and well entitled in fee simple of and to certain Lands, Messuages, Tenements and Hereditaments in his Will and hereinafter described.

After the background information, the crux of the matter is identified by such a phrase as:

> But now so it may please your Lordship that . . . which doings of him the said xxx are to the complainant's ruin and undoing and are contrary to all equity and good conscience in tender consideration whereof and forasmuch as the complainant is remediless in the premises at and by the common law.

Right at the end of the document the plaintiff asks that a subpoena be issued to the defendant requesting them to give an answer:

> May it please your lordship the premises considered to grant unto the complainant his Majesty's most gracious writ of subpoena to be directed to the said [this is the only place in the Bill of Complaint where the defendant is named as such] thereby commanding him at a certain day and under a certain pain therein to be limited personally to be and appear before your lordship in his most high and honourable court of Chancery then and there upon his corporal oath true answer make to all and singular the premises, and further to stand and abide such further orders and directions as your Lordship shall seem meet.

The plaintiff needs to prove that the case qualifies to be heard in a court of equity and so this phrase is usually used: 'so that the complainant is utterly remediless'.

The courts of equity did not rely on evidence and often the plaintiff claimed that he no longer had the crucial document that would have proved his case, with a phrase such as:

> and afterwards the said will came into the hands and possession of the defendant John who threw the same into the fire and burnt it saying the same should never rise in judgement against him.

The defendant usually opens his answer with a phrase such as:

The said defendants saving to themselves now and at all times thereafter the benefit and advantage of all exceptions to the manifest and manifold imperfections and insufficiencies and defect of the said complainant's bill of complaint for a full plain and perfect answer thereunto and unto so much thereof as concern these defendants to answer unto . . . they say and such of them for him and herself severally and respectively say as follows.

Both the plaintiff and the defendants will use a phrase such as the following after referring to any document that they are in possession of:

as by the said letter ready to be produced and shown forth more fully and at large it does and may appear.

The aim of this section of the book has been to show novices that the records are accessible, and to show those experienced with the Bills and Answers that there are many more records that can contain valuable information.

Chapter 4

THE INDEXES

This part of the book is probably not going to be the most entertaining, but it will be highly useful. The aim is to show how to identify possibly useful records in the courts of equity. It is assumed that you have access to the Internet and that you are able to visit TNA in person or to employ a specialist researcher to do so on your behalf.

BEFORE COMING TO THE NATIONAL ARCHIVES
Initially it is necessary to work out what you are looking for. Do you already believe that there is a case in a court of equity? Or are you just hoping to find something in the records? The first place to look is TNA's online catalogue Discovery. This now includes detailed searchable descriptions of some of the records, though it is always worth remembering that the vast majority of records are not indexed or described online, and paper lists at TNA have to be used. Having said that, there is an ongoing programme to provide better online descriptions of the records in Discovery, and it is always worth looking at the TNA online Research Guides for up-to-date information.

When searching for Chancery cases in Discovery use the Advanced Search, for the name and place and dates that interest you within the class reference C (for Chancery), and make a list of these records. These can then be ordered in advance if you can get to TNA or copies can be ordered for you to peruse at home.

For most of the other court of equity records it is necessary to search calendars and indexes onsite at TNA, although gradually more and more full descriptions are being included in Discovery.

Which Court Should I Look At?

Unless you have reason to look at one of the other courts, the Court of Chancery is usually the first place to look, simply because more effort has gone into the indexing and calendaring, particularly in Discovery.

You might look at the other courts if the following are relevant:

- Very poor people – try Court of Requests, but this ceased to function in 1642.
- Violence involved – try Court of Star Chamber, but this ceased to function in 1642.
- Financial case – try Court of Exchequer, remembering that after the mid-seventeenth century this court functioned in a very similar way to the Court of Chancery, and no longer specialised in financial cases relating to the Crown and the Exchequer.
- Particular geographical area – try the Palatinate courts if searching Chester, Durham or Lancaster. Remember that the Duchy of Lancaster covered Duchy properties all over the country.

CHANCERY CALENDARS AND INDEXES BEFORE 1876

The Pleadings (Bills and Answers) for the Chancery records are now well described for most periods in Discovery, however some are still only listed by the names of the principal plaintiff and defendant. For the period *c.*1649–1714 there are six concurrent series of Pleadings, and at the time of writing these are not yet all included in Discovery, however the paper calendars are on the open shelves at TNA. Work on this is continuing all the time. The paper calendars are handwritten and arranged alphabetically by the initial letter of the surname of the principal plaintiff. To make searching these a little easier there is a column for the county concerned, and it can be easier to run your eye down this column rather than the surname column. Some of these are available on microfilm in the Family History Centres of the Church of Jesus Christ of Latter-Day Saints.

The Country Depositions are listed by the name of the case in Discovery, but not by the name of the deponent. The Bernau Index, which is held at the Society of Genealogists, includes the names of the deponents for both Town and Country Depositions, and is listed in very strict alphabetical order.

The term 'Chancery Proceedings' refers to the Bills and Answers or Pleadings, and also the Interrogatories and Depositions where these are filed with the Pleadings.

There are various categories of indexing:

- Searchable online via Discovery – this can include a full description with the names of all the parties, the place and often the subject, but in some cases it only includes the surnames of the principal plaintiff and defendant.
- Paper calendars usually in IND 1 series at TNA, most need to be ordered as documents, although some are available on the open shelves.
- Bernau – microfilm at Society of Genealogists.
- Anglo American Legal Tradition (AALT) – online photos of images, with some indexing.

Work is being undertaken by TNA to include the court reference number for each case in the catalogue, making it easier to identify all documents relating to as specific case. Thus, a search for the number 'W1806 L16' gives the following references:

C 13/521/16 [W1806 L16]. Lowe v Moxon. Depositions. 1812
C 13/119/24 [W1806 L16]. Lowe v Lowe. Two   1810
answers. Plaintiffs: John Lowe and another. Defendants:
Richard Moxon, Mary Moxon (amended to Thomas
Dawes and wife Mary Dawes), Thomas Moxon, Joseph
Moxon, Nathaniel Moxon and Thomas Lowe. Amended
by an order dated 03 Jun 1806: Joseph Moxon removed
as a defendant.
C 13/105/12 [W1806 L16]. Lowe v Moxon. Two   1809

answers. Plaintiffs: John Lowe and another. Defendants:
Richard Moxon, Mary Moxon (amended to Thomas
Dawes and wife Mary Dawes), Thomas Moxon, Joseph
Moxon, Nathaniel Moxon and Thomas Lowe. Amended
by an order dated 03 Jun 1806: Joseph Moxon removed
as a defendant.

C 13/80/9 [W1806 L16]. Lowe v Lowe. Bill and answer. 1807
[MRFA two bills]. Plaintiffs: John Lowe and another.
Defendants: Richard Moxon, Mary Moxon (amended to
Thomas Dawes and wife Mary Dawes), Thomas Moxon,
Joseph Moxon, Nathaniel Moxon and Thomas Lowe.
Amended by an order dated 03 Jun 1806: Joseph Moxon
removed as a defendant. JMP.

C 13/92/13 [W1806 L16]. Lowe v Moxon. Answer.   1808
Plaintiffs: John Lowe and another. Defendants: Richard
Moxon, Mary Moxon (amended to Thomas Dawes and
wife Mary Dawes), Thomas Moxon, Joseph Moxon,
Nathaniel Moxon and Thomas Lowe. Amended by an
order dated 03 Jun 1806: Joseph Moxon removed as a
defendant.

```
C  38          Reports and Certificates

               Indexes : These are arranged alphabetically, by the
first letter of the plaintiffs' surnames.  They are broken down by
terms and for each Report or Certificate that was filed they give a
note of plaintiff, defendant and the Master to whom the case was
referred:

     Date          IND              Date          IND

   1606 - 1607     1878             1621           1892
   1607 - 1608     1879             1622           1893
   1608 - 1609     1880             1623           1894
   1609 - 1610     1881             1624           1895
   1610 - 1612     1882             1625           1896
   1611 - 1612     1883             1626           1897
   1613           1884             1627           1898
   1614           1885             1628           1899
   1615           1886             1629           1900
   1616           1887             1630           1901
   1617           1888             1631           1902
   1618           1889             1632           1903
   1619           1890             1633           1904
   1620           1891             1634           1905
```

A page from IND 1 list for C 38.

121

Class	Description	Date	Index
C 1	Early Chancery Proceedings	Richard II to Philip and Mary	Searchable online
C 2	Chancery Proceedings Series 1	Elizabeth I to Charles I	Searchable online
C 3	Chancery Proceedings Series 2	Elizabeth I to Charles I	Searchable online
C 5	Chancery Proceedings	James I to 1714	Searchable online
C 6	Chancery Proceedings	James I to 1714	Searchable online
C 7	Chancery Proceedings	James I to 1714	Searchable online
C 8	Chancery Proceedings	James I to 1714	Open shelves calendar
C 9	Chancery Proceedings	James I to 1714	Searchable online for 1st plaintiff and 1st defendant
C 10	Chancery Proceedings	James I to 1714	Searchable online for 1st plaintiff, 1st defendant and county for about half the series, also open shelves index
C 11	Chancery Proceedings	1714–58	Searchable online
C 12	Chancery Proceedings	1758–1800	Searchable online for surname only of 1st plaintiff and one defendant
C 13	Chancery Proceedings	1800–42	50 per cent and growing lists 1st plaintiff and all defendants
C 14	Chancery Proceedings	1842–52	Searchable online
C 15	Chancery Proceedings	1853–60	Searchable online
C 16	Chancery Proceedings	1861–75	Searchable online
C 21	Country Depositions	Elizabeth I to Charles I	Searchable online for 1st plaintiff and 1st defendant. Bernau for deponents
C 22	Country Depositions	1649–1714	Searchable online for 1st plaintiff and 1st defendant. Bernau for deponents
	Country Depositions	1715–1880	Filed with Proceedings
C 24	Town Depositions	1534–1853	Bernau Index
	Town Depositions	1854–80	Filed with Proceedings
C 25	Chancery Interrogatories	1598–1852	Searchable online
C 31	Chancery Affidavits	1611–1875	IND 1
C 32	Chancery Cause Books	1842–75	Included in online description for C 14, C 15 and C16
C 33	Chancery Decrees and Orders	1544–1650	AALT
C 33	Chancery Decrees and Orders	1650–1875	Calendars on open shelves
C 36	Petitions	1774–1875	IND 1
C 38	Masters' Reports	1544–1875	IND 1 from 1606
C 39	Masters' Reports (supplementary)	1580–1892	No indexes
C 41	Register of Affidavits	1615–1747	No indexes
C 78	Decree Rolls	1544–1903	AALT
C 79	Supplementary Decree Rolls	1534–1903	AALT
C 101	Masters' Accounts	1750–1850	Searchable online for all parties and places
C103–C114	Masters' Exhibits	1234–1860	Searchable online
C117–C126	Masters' Documents	17th to 19th centuries	IND 1
C 276	Account ledgers	1726–1841	Calendars on open shelves
C 278	Account journals	1725–1841	No index

A typical page from a calendar of Chancery Orders and Decrees, 1655.

Where the list refers to IND 1, this is to index or calendar volumes that need to be ordered as documents. There is no online reference to these, although work is being done to incorporate these references into Discovery. Until then, there is a list at TNA that can be used by asking the TNA staff for it. This matches up the appropriate index volume to the period and subject being searched.

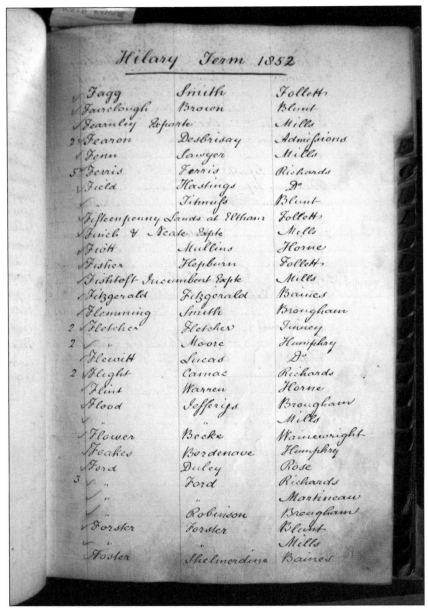

A typical page from a calendar of Chancery Masters' Reports.

EXCHEQUER COURT CALENDARS AND INDEXES

It sometimes feels as though the Court of the Exchequer has been neglected as far as indexing and good online descriptions are concerned. The easiest way into these records is through the Depositions by Commission in class E 134. These were listed and indexed by the names of the parties many years ago in print, and this list is now available online in Discovery from 1558 to 1820. The other records are only available by searching in person at TNA.

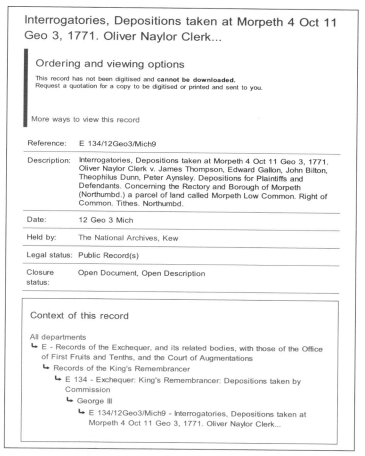

Interrogatories, Depositions taken at Morpeth 4 Oct 11 Geo 3, 1771. Oliver Naylor Clerk...

Ordering and viewing options

This record has not been digitised and **cannot be downloaded.**
Request a quotation for a copy to be digitised or printed and sent to you.

More ways to view this record

Reference:	E 134/12Geo3/Mich9
Description:	Interrogatories, Depositions taken at Morpeth 4 Oct 11 Geo 3, 1771. Oliver Naylor Clerk v. James Thompson, Edward Gallon, John Bilton, Theophilus Dunn, Peter Aynsley. Depositions for Plaintiffs and Defendants. Concerning the Rectory and Borough of Morpeth (Northumbd.) a parcel of land called Morpeth Low Common. Right of Common. Tithes. Northumbd.
Date:	12 Geo 3 Mich
Held by:	The National Archives, Kew
Legal status:	Public Record(s)
Closure status:	Open Document, Open Description

Context of this record

All departments
↳ E - Records of the Exchequer, and its related bodies, with those of the Office of First Fruits and Tenths, and the Court of Augmentations
  ↳ Records of the King's Remembrancer
    ↳ E 134 - Exchequer: King's Remembrancer: Depositions taken by Commission
      ↳ George III
        ↳ E 134/12Geo3/Mich9 - Interrogatories, Depositions taken at Morpeth 4 Oct 11 Geo 3, 1771. Oliver Naylor Clerk...

A typical Discovery entry from Exchequer Depositions by Composition, E 134.

The Bills and Answers are reasonably well listed in the calendars on the open shelves.

Reference	Description	Date	Index
E 112	Pleadings	Elizabeth to Victoria	Open shelves calendar
E 123	Entry books of Decrees and Orders	1559–1606	Open shelves calendar
E 124	Entry books of Orders	1603–25	Open shelves calendar
E 125	Entry books of Orders	1625–61	Open shelves calendar
E 126	Entry books of Decrees	1605–1841	Open shelves calendar and IND 1
E 127	Entry book of Orders	1661–1841	IND 1
E 133	Barons' Depositions (London)	Elizabeth to 1841	Online by surnames of parties
E 134	Depositions taken by commission (Country)	Elizabeth to Victoria	Online, full names of parties but not deponents
E 140	Exhibits	1319–1841	Online, surnames of parties, description of Exhibits
E 194	Reports	1648–1841	IND 1
E 217	Account books	1675–1841	No index
E 219	Exhibits and working papers	1625–1841	No index

COURT OF REQUESTS CALENDARS AND INDEXES

These records are well worth looking at, as this court dealt with cases brought by poorer people, however accessing most of them entails searching paper calendars and indexes on the open shelves at TNA. Any Depositions that have survived are filed with the Pleadings.

Reference	Description	Date	Index
REQ 1	Process books such as Orders and Decrees, notebooks, Affidavits	1453–1642	No index
REQ 2	Pleadings	1485–1601	Some searchable online before 1553, others via calendars on open shelves with index
REQ 2	Pleadings	1603–42	Open shelves calendar with index
REQ 3	Miscellanea, unsorted proceedings and other records	1485–1642	No index
REQ 4	Documents of Shakespearean interest		3 cases listed online

COURT OF STAR CHAMBER CALENDARS AND INDEXES

The records are worth looking at for pure entertainment value. To qualify for this court it was necessary to prove that there was violence involved, particularly a riot. The amount of violence was usually exaggerated, but the records do make for interesting reading. The Interrogatories and Depositions are filed with the pleadings. The Orders and Decrees have all been lost. There are no Affidavits, Petitions or Masters' Records.

Reference	Description	Date	Index
STAC 1	Pleadings	Edward IV–Henry VII	Online by plaintiff, defendant, subject, place and county
STAC 2	Pleadings	Henry VIII	Online by plaintiff, defendant, subject, place and county
STAC 3	Pleadings	Edward VI	Online by plaintiff, defendant, subject, place and county
STAC 4	Pleadings	Philip and Mary	Online by plaintiff, defendant, subject, place and county
STAC 5	Pleadings	Elizabeth	By plaintiff and defendant only
STAC 7	Pleadings	Elizabeth (supplementary)	Open shelves calendar
STAC 8	Pleadings	James I	By plaintiff, defendant and county
STAC 9	Pleadings	Charles I	By plaintiff, defendant subject, place and county
STAC 10	Miscellanea	*c.*1600	Searchable online for about 10 per cent, the remainder are unsorted

COURT OF DUCHY OF LANCASTER CALENDARS AND INDEXES

The Duchy had lands in counties as far from Lancashire as Somerset, Yorkshire, Suffolk and London which are all included and so this is an important court to be searched. The only section that is searchable online is DL 4.

No.	Reign.	Plaintiffs.	Defendants.	Premises, and Matters in Dispute.	Places.	Counties.
10.	2 & 3 Phil. & Mar.	Richard Haydok claiming by Deed from Richard Grene to the Plaintiff, and to Thomas Buckley, Clerk, Parfon of Brynhill, to the Ufe of the Will of the faid Richard Grene.	The Right Honourable Sir Thomas Stanley, Knight, Lord Mountegle, Adam Holden, his Bailiff, and others, the faid Lord Mountegle claiming the Reverfion in Chorley, as Efcheat by the Death of Richard Grene without Heir.	Difputed Title to Meffuages, Lands, and Appurtenances, with Interrogatories and Depofitions thereon, and therein particularly of the Houfe called GreneHall in Heapey.	Hepaye. Chorley.	Lancafhire.

I. & J.

No.	Reign.	Plaintiffs.	Defendants.	Premises, and Matters in Dispute.	Places.	Counties.
1.	1 & 2 Phil. & Mar.	Chriftopher Ingham otherwife Yngham, and Margaret his Wife, claiming by Leafe from Sir Richard Townley, Knight, deceafed.	Richard Towneley, claiming the Reverfion as Heir Male of the Body of Sir John Townley, Knight, deceafed.	Difputed Title to a Meffuage, Lands, and Tenements, and particularly a Houfe called a Cote, and Lands called Golden Flatt, the Cowecroft, the Croft on the Backfyde of the Barne, and Whicken Lands, Afshen, Stolles, and Carre.	Clevecher.	Lancafhire.
2.	2 & 3 Phil. & Mar.	Walter Jennings otherwife Gennings, claiming by Leafe from King Henry the 8th, to the Plaintiff, and to Johan and Mary his Daughters.	John Hinton claiming in Fee by Knights Service, as of the Manor of Cranborne.	Difputed Title to a Cottage and Land, Parcel of a Farm called Wodmere, in Peterfham, with Interrogatories and Depofitions thereon; and particularly of Abrell Croft, in the Tithing of Peterfham, as being within the Duchy of York, Parcel of the Dukedom of York, and holden of the Duke of York, as of his Manor of Cranbourne.	Kingftone Lacey Manor. Peterfham. Wymborne Mynfter. Cranborne Manor. Abelcrofte.	Dorfetfhire.

K.

No.	Reign.	Plaintiffs.	Defendants.	Premises, and Matters in Dispute.	Places.	Counties.
1.	1 & 2 Phil. & Mar.	William Kylner.	Robert Barrowe, Richard Fell, and others.	Tortious Poffeffion of Meadow Land and Pafture.	Cartmell.	Lancafhire.
2.	1 & 2 Phil. & Mar.	Katheryn Kyrkeby late Wife of John Kyrkebye, deceafed. The King and Queen. See R.	Richard Seelle.	Tortious Poffeffion and Detention of Title Deeds relating to Three Capital Meffuages and 200 Acres of Meadow Land.	Lawwycke.	Lancafhire.

M.

No.	Reign.	Plaintiffs.	Defendants.	Premises, and Matters in Dispute.	Places.	Counties.
1.	1 & 2 Phil. & Mar.	Sir Richard Mullyneux, Knight. Et e contra.	Edmund Holme, George Holme, and others.	Difputed Title to Mofs and other Lands, and to Right of Turbary in the Wafte Ground called Male Mofs.	Maghull. Male Mofs. Hormfchurche.	Lancafhire.
2.	1 & 2 Phil. & Mar.	Robert Metham.	Sir Richard Chomley, Knight, and others.	Illegal Diftrefs of Goods and Chattles, the Plaintiff alledging that he was feized of and in a Parcel of Ground called Stayndayle, being of the Demefnes of the Manor Houfe of Lockton, and of a Houfe called a Hay Howfe, and that an unlawful Pain was laid by the Four Fofters of Fee of the Chace of Pykarynglithe that the Plaintiff fhould take down the faid Hay Howfe before the next Attachment Court, or elfe forfeit Forty Shillings; and that it was prefented at the next Court by the faid Four Fofters, that he had not fo done, wherefore he was affeered to pay 40s., which having been demanded, and by him refufed, the Defendants diftrained, and took away his Goods and Chattles.	Stayndale. Lockton Manor. Rokyfby. Pykarynglithe. Pykarynglithe Chace. Snaynton Court in the Liberties of Pykarynglith.	Yorkfhire.

A typical calendar of Depositions from the Duchy of Lancaster.

Reference	Description	Date	Index
DL 1	Pleadings	1509–1835	IND 1 and open shelves calendar
DL 3	Pleadings, Depositions, examinations	1509–58	Open shelves calendar
DL 4	Pleadings, Depositions, examinations	1558–1818	Searchable online
DL 5	Entry books of Decrees and Orders	1474–1872	IND 1
DL 6	Draft Decrees	1509–1810	No index
DL 8	Draft injunctions	1614–1794	No index
DL 9	Affidavits, reports, certificates, Orders	1561–1857	No index

COURT OF PALATINATE OF LANCASTER CALENDARS AND INDEXES

This court covers just the county of Lancashire.

Reference	Description	Date	Index
PL 6	Bills	1419–1853	Searchable online 1419–1611, then IND 1
PL 7	Answers	1474–1858	IND 1 1628–1676
PL 8	Replications, rejoinders	1601–1856	IND 1 1628–1676
PL 9	Affidavits	1610–1836	No index
PL 10	Depositions	1581–1854	No index
PL 11	Entry books of Decrees and Orders	1524–1863	No index
PL 12	Exhibits	1653–1864	Searchable online
PL 14	Miscellaneous including Pleadings	1377–1896	Some in IND 1

COURT OF PALATINATE OF CHESTER CALENDARS AND INDEXES

This court covers just the counties of Chester and Flint.

Reference	Description	Date	Index
CHES 14	Entry books of Decrees and Orders	1562–1830	Internal indexes in some volumes arranged by name of principal plaintiff
CHES 15	Pleadings inc. Depositions	1509–George IV	IND 1 for 1760–1820
CHES 16	Pleadings (refer to loans and debts rather than to land)	1559–1762	No index
CHES 12	Unpublished Depositions	Elizabeth to 18th century	4 bundles only

COURT OF PALATINATE OF DURHAM CALENDARS AND INDEXES

This court covers just the county of Durham.

Reference	Description	Date	Index
DURH 1	Affidavits	1657–1812	No index
DURH 2	Pleadings	1576–1840	No index
DURH 4	Entry books of Decrees and Orders	1633–1898	Some internal indexes
DURH 5	Original Decrees, Orders and reports	1613–1778	No index
DURH 7	Interrogatories, Depositions	1557–1804	No index

Please be aware that as full catalogue descriptions are added to Discovery for more classes, the above lists for all the courts, particularly the Court of Chancery, will become out of date, if not totally superfluous.

COURT OF CHANCERY AFTER 1876

There is no standard way into the equity records after 1876, but the cases can be as interesting and useful to family historians as the records before that date, so it is worth persevering with them. The process was similar, with a case starting with a Bill of Complaint and moving through Answers, Interrogatories, Depositions, Masters' Reports, Affidavits, Petitions, etc. Before 1876 the easiest way to find a Chancery case is via TNA's online catalogue Discovery. After 1876 this method is not possible, but there are other means of getting at the records. Many were reported in *The Times* and some in local newspapers. Notification of some was given in the *London Gazette* which lists outstanding cases in supplements at the end of each edition. A typical list includes the parties' names, the date the case started, the date and nature of the last transaction, and the date of Orders and Reports.

For example the supplement for 1890 includes:

Shelton v. Kidman, case number 1871 S141, the account of the infant Plaintiff, William Thomas Kidman, and Marian Kidman, Elizabeth Kidman, and Isabel Edith Kidman, the infant children of Mary Ann Shelton, formerly Mary Ann Kidman,

Index to titles of Accounts (with cross references).	Year in which the Account was opened.	Date and nature of last transaction.	Date of Order or other Authority directing last transaction to be made.
CHANCERY—continued.			
Shipley, see Kishere v. Fitzgerald			
Shipp, see Richard Nurse			
Shirley v. Earl Ferrers, and Earl Ferrers v. Ward, in Master Holford's office	1796	18th May, 1797. Payment out	Ord. 23rd Jan., 1797, and Rept. 23rd March, 1797
Shirriff, see Willoby			
Shore, see Humble v. Shore			
Shore v. Lee	1833	28th Nov., 1871. Investment	Ord. 22nd Nov., 1871
Shore, Lydia, see Humble v. Shore			
Shore, Alice, see Court v. Jeffery			
Short, Jane, see Elizabeth Stacey			
Shotter, Gawen, see Annie Drummond			
Showler, see Briggs v. Wilson			
Shrapnell, Henry Squires, see Leith v. Mant			
Shreeve v. Shreeve	1863	9th May, 1865. Payment out	Ord. 8th July, 1864, and Certe. fd. 15th Mar., 1865
Shrewsbury and Birmingham Railway, see Bird v. Breese			
Shrewsbury and Birmingham Railway Company, ex parte the, in the matter of the Shrewsbury and Birmingham Railway Act, 1846	1847	28th March, 1854. Investment	Ord. 9th Feb., 1854
Shrewsbury and Hereford Railway Company, ex parte the, the account of Charles Price, Gentleman	1851	31st July, 1851. Lodgment	Said Railway Act, 1846
Shrieve, Mary, see Rogers v. Rogers			
Shropshire Union Railways and Canal Company, ex parte the Forton School Fund	1856	Not dealt with ...	Ord. 11th May, 1856, re Forton School Fund
Shuck, see Waldron v. Boulter			
Shuckburgh, Mary A., see re Nicholett			
Shuthonger Common, see Tewkesbury and Malvern Railway Company			
Shuttleworth v. Greaves	1833	24th Aug., 1843. Payment.out	Ord. 20th Dec., 1842 Rept. 16th Aug., 1843
Shuttleworth v. Howarth, the account of the descendants of John Kay	1844	17th Nov., 1849. Payment out	Ord. 10th Aug., 1839, and Rept. 14th June, 1844
Sibery, Edward, in the matter of the trusts of the will of Edward Sibery, deceased, so far as the same relate to the share of the children of the said testator's daughter Harriot Bates	1868	3rd June, 1869. Payment out	Ord. 12th Dec., 1868
Sibley, see Robert Owen			
Sidden v. Forster, and Sidden v. Lediard, the account of the creditors of Robert Woolley	1841	Not dealt with ...	Ord. 2nd Aug., 1841
Sidebotham, see Stockport and Woodley Railway			
Silk v. Dimsdale, the account of the unsatisfied creditors of Christopher Thompson	1819	Not dealt with ...	Ord. 29th June, 1818, in Silk v. Pryme
Silk, Ann, an infant legatee...	1826	23rd Jan., 1827. Investment	Act 36 Geo. III, c. 52
Silk, Clare, an infant legatee	1826	23rd Jan., 1827. Investment	Act 36 Geo. III, c. 52
Sill v. Boden	1865	Not dealt with ...	Ord. 23rd Jan., 1865, and Afft. fd. 25th March, 1865
Silver v. Silver	1838	2nd Dec., 1867. Payment out	Ord. 25th June, 1867
Silvester, see Steedman v. Silvester			
Simmonds, see Stiff v. Simmonds			
Simms, see Turner v. Simms			
Simpkin v. Waldram, 1866, S., 236... ...	1871	20th Mar., 1873. Lodgment	Ord. 14th Feb., 1867, and Certe. fd. 8th March, 1873
Simpson, see Citizens' Bank of Lousiana v. Simpson			
Simpson v. Allison, the account of the children of Joseph Barker	1863	Not dealt with ...	Ord. 29th May, 1863
Simpson v. Gutteridge, the life account of the plaintiff James Simpson	1821	25th May, 1822. Payment out	Ord. 29th May, 1822
Simpson, Mary Ann, see Prince v. Cooper			
Simpson, Palgrave, see Tarbuck v. Tarbuck			
Simpson, Palgrave, see Tarbuck v. Greenall			
Sinclair, Lord, v. Ballantyne	1819	17th Aug., 1832. Transfer out	Ord. 26th July, 1832

T 2

A London Gazette supplement showing Chancery cases.

PURSUANT to a Judgment of the High Court of Justice, Chancery Division. made in an action in the matter of the estate of Henry Smith, deceased, Smith against Smith, 1881, S. 5540, the creditors of Henry Smith, late of Broom Lodge, Hatfield, in the county of York, Auctioneer and Valuer, who died in or about the month of January, 1881, are, on or before the 10th day of March, 1882, to send by post, pre-paid, to Mr. Edward Thomas Moore, a member of the firm of Broomhead, Wightman, and Moore, of Bank-chambers, George-street, Sheffield, in the county of York, the Solicitor of the plaintiff, Joseph Smith, who, with the defendant, Hannah Smith, Widow, are the executors of the said Henry Smith, deceased, their Christian and surnames. addresses and descriptions, the full particulars of their claims, a statement of their accounts, and the nature of the securities (if any) held by them, or in default thereof they will be peremptorily excluded from the benefit of the said Judgment. Every creditor holding any security is to produce the same before the Honourable Mr. Justice Chitty, at his chambers, situate in the Royal Courts of Justice, Strand, Middlesex, on Friday, the 24th day of March, 1882, at eleven of the clock in the forenoon, being the time appointed for adjudicating on the claims.—Dated this 9th day of February, 1882.

PURSUANT to a Judgment of the High Court of Justice, Chancery Division, in an action in the matter of the estates of Samuel Lover and Mary Jane Lover respectively deceased, Wilhelm Marius Schmid against Richard William Waudby Griffin and another, 1881, L., No. 3038, the creditors of Samuel Lover, late of Clear View, St. Lawrence Valley, in the Island of Jersey, formerly of Sevenoaks, in the county of Kent, and 2, St. Mark's-villas, St. Helier's, Jersey aforesaid, Esq., deceased, who died on or about the 6th day of July, 1868, are, on or before the 11th day of March, 1882, to send by post, prepaid, to Mr. George Andrews, of Weymouth, in the county of Dorset, a member of the firm of Andrews, Barrett, and Andrews, of the same place, the Solicitors for the defendants, the legal personal representatives of the deceased, their Christian and surnames, addresses and descriptions, the full particulars of their claims, a statement of their accounts, and the nature of the securities (if any) held by them, or in default thereof they will be peremptorily excluded from the benefit of the said Judgment. Every creditor holding any security is to produce the same before Mr. Justice Chitty, at his chambers, in the Royal Courts of Justice, Strand, Middlesex, on Monday, the 20th day of March, 1882, at twelve of the clock at noon, being the time appointed for adjudicating on the claims.—Dated this 6th day of February, 1882.

PURSUANT to a Judgment of the High Court of Justice, Chancery Division, in an action in the matter of the estate of Samuel Lover and Mary Jane Lover respectively, deceased, Wilhelm Marius Schmid against Richard William Waudby Griffin and another, 1881, L., No. 3038, the creditors of Mary Jane Lover, late of Fitzroy Lodge, Bournemouth, in the county of Hants, Widow, and previous to her death residing at Weymouth, in the county of Dorset, who died on or about the 15th day of November, 1880, are, on or before the 11th day of March, 1882, to send by post, prepaid, to Mr. George Andrews, of Weymouth, in the county of Dorset, a member of the firm of Andrews, Barrett, and Andrews, of the same place, Solicitors for the defendants, the executors of the deceased, Mary Jane Lover, their Christian and surnames, addresses and descriptions, the full particulars of their claims, a statement of their accounts, and the nature of the securities (if any) held by them, or in default thereof they will be peremptorily excluded from the benefit of the said Judgment. Every creditor holding any security is to produce the same before Mr. Justice Chitty, at his chambers, in the Royal Courts of Justice, Strand, Middlesex, on Monday, the 20th day of March, 1882, at twelve of the clock at noon, being the time appointed for adjudicating upon the said claims.—Dated this 6th day of February, 1882.

PURSUANT to a Judgment of the High Court of Justice, Chancery Division, made in the matter of the estate of John Porter, deceased, and in an action Potter against Potter, 1880, P., No. 0850, the creditors of John Potter, late of 127, Southwark Bridge-road, in the county of Surrey, Coach and Cart Wheelwright, who died in or about the month of January, 1876, are, on or before the 4th day of March, 1882, to send by post, prepaid, to Mr. Robert Emmott Large, of 13, South-square, Gray's-inn, in the county of Middlesex, the Solicitor of the plaintiff, one of the executors of the deceased, their Christian and surnames, addresses and descriptions, the full particulars of their claims, a statement of their accounts, and the nature of the securities (if any) held by them, or in default thereof they will be peremptorily excluded from the benefit of the said Judgment. Every creditor holding any security is to produce the same before his Lordship, the Honourable Mr. Justice Fry, at his chambers, situated No. 12, Staple-inn, Holborn, Middlesex, on Monday, the 13th day of March

1882, at twelve o'clock at noon, being the time appointed for adjudicating on the claims.—Dated this 7th day of February, 1882.

John Henry Gent, Deceased.

PURSUANT to a Judgment, dated 5th August, 1880, in an action re Gent-Davis v. Harris, 1880, G., 920, all persons claiming to be nephews and nieces of the testator, John Henry Gent, late of Fortis Green, Finchley, in the county of Middlesex, Merchant, deceased, being children of the said testator's brothers, Charles James Gent and Walter George Gent, and his sisters, Alice Henrietta Davis, Diana Olivia Harris, and Clara (or Clara Julia) West, are, by their Solicitors, on or before the 10th day of June, 1882, to come in and prove their claims at the chambers of the Honourable Mr. Justice Fry, situate at No. 12, Staple-inn, Holborn, in the county of Middlesex, or in default thereof they will be peremptorily excluded from the benefit of the said Judgment. Tuesday, the 20th day of June, 1882, at twelve o'clock at noon, at the said chambers, is appointed for hearing and adjudicating upon the said claims. Notice.—Under the said testator's will, the said nephews and nieces are legatees, and entitled to a share of residue, but the said will contains a proviso that they are to come forward and claim their shares of residue or other interests within two years from the publication of advertisement or notice, and if no claim be made within such time, the person or persons so in default are to lose and be deprived of all beneficial interest under the said will.—Dated this 8th day of February, 1882.

PURSUANT to a Judgment of the High Court of Justice, Chancery Division, made in an action in the matter of the estate of Thomas Dowker Woodall, deceased, Woodall v. Woodall, 1881, W., No. 4779, the creditors of Thomas Dowker Woodall, late of Scarborough, in the county of York, Esq., who died in or about the month of January, 1838, are, on or before the 18th day of March, 1882, to send by post, prepaid, to Mr. Frank Milner Russell, of No. 4, Bedford-row, in the county of Middlesex, a member of the firm of Messrs. Collyer-Bristow, Withers, and Russell, of the same place, the Solicitors of the defendant, their Christian and surnames, addresses and descriptions, the full particulars of their claims, a statement of their accounts, and the nature of the securities (if any) held by them, or in default thereof they will be peremptorily excluded from the benefit of the said Judgment. Every creditor holding any security is to produce the same before the Honourable Mr. Justice Fry, at his chambers, situated No. 12, Staple-inn, Holborn, Middlesex, on Friday, the 31st day of March, 1882, at twelve of the clock at noon, being the time appointed for adjudicating on the claims.—Dated this 6th day of February, 1882.

PURSUANT to an Order of the late High Court of Justice, Chancery Division, made in an action in the matter of the estate of Louisa Payne, Widow, deceased, Pettit against Rumball, 1882, P., No. 31, the creditors of Louisa Payne, late of Brooklyn-road, Shepherd's Bush, in the county of Middlesex, Widow, who died in or about the month of July, 1881, are, on or before the 10th day of March, 1882, to send by post, prepaid, to Mr. William Searle Parker, of the firm of Messrs. Parker, of 17, Bedford-row, in the county of Middlesex, the Solicitors of the defendant, the executor of the said Louisa Payne, deceased, their Christian and surnames, addresses and descriptions, the full particulars of their claims, a statement of their accounts, and the nature of the securities (if any) held by them, or in default thereof they will be peremptorily excluded from the benefit of the said Order. Every creditor holding any security is to produce the same before the Honourable Mr. Justice Fry, at his chambers, situated at No. 12, Staple-inn, Holborn, Middlesex, on Tuesday, the 21st day of March, 1882, at twelve o'clock at noon, being the time appointed for adjudicating on the claims.—Dated this 8th day of February, 1882.

PURSUANT to a Judgment of the High Court of Justice, Chancery Division, made in an action in the matter of the estate of William Stannage, late of Leicester, in the county of Leicester, deceased, Boot against Stannage, 1881, S., No. 5526, the creditors of William Stannage, late of Leicester, in the county of Leicester, Labourer, deceased, who died in or about the month of March, 1881, are, on or before the 18th day of March, 1882, to send by post, prepaid, to Lionel Percy Chamberlain, of No. 14, New-street, Leicester, in the county of Leicester, the Solicitor of the defendant, their Christian and surnames, addresses and descriptions, the full particulars of their claims, a statement of their accounts, and the nature of the securities (if any) held by them, or in default thereof they will be peremptorily excluded from the benefit of the said Judgment. Every creditor holding any security is to produce the same before the Honourable Mr. Justice Fry, at his chambers, situate at No. 12, Staple-inn, Holborn, Middlesex, on Monday, the 3rd day of April, 1882, at twelve o'clock at noon, being the time appointed for adjudicating on the claims.—Dated this 3rd day of February, 1882.

The London Gazette *showing Chancery cases.*

deceased, subject to duty was started in 1874, with an order of 24th January 1874.

Many cases listed in the supplements have remained unresolved for many years, such as the case of Shellaber v Maud which started in 1766 and was still listed amongst the dormant cases in 1902. The *London Gazette*, 4 December 1888, includes:

PURSUANT to a Judgment, dated 5th August, 1880, in an action re Gent-Davis v. Harris, 1880 G 920, all persons claiming to be nephews and nieces of the testator, John Henry Gent, late of Fortis Green, Finchley, in the county of Middlesex, Merchant, deceased, being children of the said testator's brothers, Charles James, gentleman and Walter George, gentleman, and his sisters, Alice Henrietta Davis, Diana Olivia Harris, and Clara (or Clara Julia) West are, by their Solicitors, on or before the 10th day of June, 1882, to come in and prove their claims at the chambers of the Honourable Mr. Justice Fry, situate at No. 12, Staple Inn, Holborn, in the county of Middlesex, or in default thereof they will be peremptorily excluded from the benefit of the said Judgment. Tuesday, the 20th day of June, 1882, at twelve o'clock at noon, at the said chambers, is appointed for hearing and adjudicating upon the said claims. NOTICE—Under the said testator's will, the said nephews, and nieces are legatees, and entitled to a share of residue, but the said will contains a proviso that they are to come forward and claim their shares of residue or other interests within two years from the publication of advertisement or notice, and if no claim be made within such time, the person or persons so in default are to lose and be deprived of all beneficial interest under the said will.—Dated this 8th day of February, 1882.

If a case cannot be found from either of these sources, the calendars of the Orders and Decrees should be the next area of research. As with those for the earlier period before 1876, these are on the open shelves at TNA.

Chapter 5

SAMPLE CASES

The sample cases featured in this chapter have been looked at in rather more detail than the cases that have been referred to thus far. They illustrate some of the most common reasons for a case being brought to the courts of equity. The information given here is only a snapshot of the detail that is provided in the records.

LOANS AND DEBTS

The case of Theodosia Bligh is interesting in that she was from an eminent family, as were many of those who appear in the records of the courts of equity.[1] However the case illustrates one of the most common types of case: that of debts unpaid.

The case is brought in 1714 by Nicholas Shults of the parish of St Martin-in-the-Fields in the county of Middlesex, perukemaker, Henry Hyde of the parish of St James Westminster in the said county of Middlesex Innkeeper, and Richard Stapler of the parish of St Anne Westminster in the said county of Middlesex, coach-maker. The nub of this case is that the plaintiffs are owed money by Lord Cornbury, now deceased. In Lord Cornbury's will he left the majority of his estate to his sister Lady Theodosia Hyde, who has since married John Bligh (both are defendants). The plaintiffs claim that Edward Earl of Clarendon (Lord Cornbury's father), Henry Earl of Rochester and John Bligh have refused to pay the creditors of the deceased Lord Cornbury, sometimes pretending that there is not sufficient money as Lord Cornbury was indebted to Edward Earl of Clarendon and Henry Earl of Rochester.

The ancestry and family of Theodosia Bligh is fairly readily available online and in books such as *Burke's Peerage*, and indeed Queen Anne was her cousin, being the daughter of her grandfather Henry 2nd Earl of Clarendon's sister Anne Hyde. What is not so readily available is the insight that this Chancery case gives into the way of life of the Clarendon family and others of their social standing. We are told that:

> Lord Cornbury was in his life time and at the time of his death indebted unto your orator Nicholas Shults for three periwigs in the sum of twenty-one pounds ten shillings.
>
> And was also indebted unto your orator the said Henry Hyde for keeping several coach horses hunting horses and other horses at livery, and for a coach horse sold to his Lordship and for diet and provisions for his Lordship's groom's boy during his illness and for candles burnt in the stables and for other things provided and done by his Lordship's order in the sum of one hundred twenty-two pounds fourteen shillings and nine-pence
>
> And also unto your orator Richard Stapler as his coach and coach-harness maker for goods wares and merchandise sold and delivered by the said Richard Stapler in the way and business of his trade as aforesaid in the sum of thirty-four pounds thirteen shillings and ten pence.

Learning that Henry Hyde the innkeeper had provided food for Lord Cornbury's groom's boy whilst he was ill gives us a touch of real people and real life, and of course hearing that whilst the boy was ill candles were burnt in the stable suggests a small boy being afraid of the dark. We all know that men of standing wore a wig at this date, but that Lord Cornbury owed £21 10s. for three wigs shows that one wig was not enough, and will also provide useful information for social historians by outlining the price of wigs in the early eighteenth century.

The value of the personal estate of Lord Cornbury is not surprising, however, although the courts of equity had jurisdiction over England and Wales, it is notable that his estates included feu duties in Scotland, as well as:

> several coaches chariots chairs coach-horses hunting horses and other horses, and of several diamond rings and other rings plate jewels rich embroidered cloths and other cloths linen and fine lace, and of a curious collection of books pictures and prints, and of several gold and silver watches gold snuff boxes and other boxes, and things to the value of six thousand pounds and upwards.

Many cases in the courts of equity concern simple debts like this one, and although they do not usually provide much genealogical information, the type of debts, the amount of the debts and the type of people who owed and were owed money all shed a light on the social history of the country. This also illustrates the difficulty tradesmen had in persuading those in the aristocracy to pay their bills.

PROBATE DISPUTE

In a case brought by the Trustees of the British Museum against the White family we are told that in his will, William White left the majority of his real and personal estate to Henry Leigh and John Bull in trust first for his wife Caroline Avis White (née Leigh) if she remained unmarried, and then for his son William John White, after whose death the trustees were to sell everything and give the proceeds to the Trustees of the British Museum.[2]

Although his wife Caroline survived him, his son William John White died as an infant. Further to this, the Museum Trustees claimed that in his will William White bequeathed his mother Catherine White £5,000 3 per cent annuities (part of £5,959 17s. 9d. bequeathed to her by her own husband in his will of 1799 and which William would have inherited on his mother's death) and £2,000 East India stock. They claimed that because of this Catherine the mother thereby relinquished her claim on the interest from a further

£20,000 consolidated 3 per cent annuities which formed part of her marriage settlement. However, Catherine claimed the full £5,959 17s. 9d. as well as a life interest in the £20,000. The Museum Trustees said that she was bound to choose between them. They felt that if she chose the life interest in the £20,000 then they were entitled to compensation

In essence, the Trustees to the British Museum claimed they were entitled to the residuary personal estate of the Testator after Caroline Avis White's death. This case is typical in that there is a dispute when the unexpected happens. William White married in 1821, but died in 1823, leaving his mother alive, his wife alive and his young son alive. This young son then dies. In dispute are the terms of the marriage settlement of the mother of 1798, the marriage settlement of the wife of 1821 and what should happen given that his son and heir has died.

The entire will is quoted word for word:

I William White of Tavistock Square described in the Bank Books as of Store Street Bedford Square London hereby revoking all former Wills do thus devise that my body be buried at Newington as speedily and with as little expense as may be possible at the same time charging that I be placed in a strong lead coffin and enveloped completely in quick lime. My estate at Wildern in Hampshire my houses at Cowes and all other my real property I devise to my wife for life, if she continue unmarried but if she marry that estate shall immediately cease and the next in remainder take effect which next remainder is to my son for his life with remainder to Henry Leigh of Yarmouth Isle of Wight Esquire and the Reverend John Bull of Christ Church Oxford and their heirs in trust to preserve contingent remainders with remainder to the heirs male of the body of my said son with remainder to the heirs female of the body of my said son with remainder to the said Henry Leigh and John Bull their heirs and assigns in trust to sell the same and for that purpose may make conveyances give receipts reimburse themselves and do all other necessary and usual acts and shall pay the money issuing from such sale unto the hands of the Trustees for the time being of the British Museum or as they the said Trustees shall appoint.

I the above written William White of my personal property do hereby thus dispose, to my wife Caroline Avis White I give all my moveables as plate linen furniture etc. to use them as she pleases and to be no ways accountable for them in case she dies without marrying again yet the property of them to be vested in my Executors who shall in case of her so marrying a second time as aforesaid compel delivery of all and singular the things which shall be delivered unto her use according to this bequest and at their discretion shall make sale of the same and apply the money as the residue of my property hereinafter devised.

Also I devise that my mother may and will choose what articles she pleases out of the same moveables which I possess at my decease and take them entirely at her own disposal. Five thousand pounds three per cent consolidated settled on my mother Catherine White on her marriage to which I am entitled in reversion bequeath to the said Catherine White her executors administrators and assigns, or if she refuse to let twenty thousand pounds (£20,000) three per cent consolidated bank annuities now standing in our joint names be considered as the part residue of my property, this bequest shall be void.

There then follow various legacies to be paid from the residue, with details of why he is giving the residuary estate to the British Museum, after his wife's death:

after her decease my executors shall immediately then transfer and pay over all the residue of my property and monies vested as aforesaid and the stocks in which such residue or monies be vested unto the Governors for the time being of that National Institution the British Museum or as they shall direct or appoint *for from the nation my property came* and when I leave my son enough to be a farmer he has that which may make him as happy and respectable as he could be in any station and it is my charge that he be brought up.

The conditions to this bequest show us something of the character of William White. He very much wants to be recognised as a major benefactor to the museum:

The money and property so bequeathed to the British Museum I wish to be employed in building or improving upon the said institution and that round the frieze of some part of such building or if this money is otherwise employed then over or upon that which has so employed it in the words Gulielmus White arm Britannia dicabit 18 be carved or words of that import, it is a little vanity of no harm and may tempt others to follow my example in thinking more of the nation and less of themselves.

There is indeed a frieze there today, although the wording is slightly different to that dictated by William White in his will:

ERECTED FROM FUNDS BEQUEATHED TO THE BRITISH MUSEUM FROM WILLIAM WHITE A.D. MDCCCLXXXIII

As with all Chancery cases, there is a good amount of incidental interesting information. First we see that although the White Wing at the Museum was not built until 1883, the case was brought in 1824 very soon after the death of William White.

We are given the date of death of William White as 13 May 1823, and told that he left an only son John White, his mother Catherine White and his wife Caroline Avis White. We are then told that John White the son died intestate unmarried and under the age of 21, and that his heir at law was George White. On this occasion the Chancery records are unhelpful in that the relationship of George

White the heir at law to William and his son John is never given. According to the Trustees of the Museum, George White, Catherine (the mother) and Caroline (the wife) were now trying to pretend that the will was somehow at fault and that the bequest of the entire residuary estate to the Museum was invalid.

> And these Defendants have been informed and believe that the said William White did not sign seal or publish or acknowledge his signature on the said Will in the presence of any or either of the persons whose names or name are or is subscribed as witnesses or witness thereto save only as herein after mentioned but that after he had signed and sealed the same he requested John Hounslow and Mary Bristow (two of the persons whose names are subscribed thereto as purporting to be witnesses to the signing and sealing of the said Will by the said William White) to sign their names thereto which they accordingly did but that he did not inform them or either of them what paper it was which they so signed.

And that at the time when they so signed the same they were entirely ignorant that the same was the Testator's Will or any testamentary writing.

> And that some time after the said paper writing or Will had been so signed by the said John Hounslow and Mary Bristow the said Testator carried the same to Thomas Badcock (the other person whose name is subscribed thereto as purporting to witness the signing and sealing of the said Will by the said William White) and requested him to sign the same which he accordingly did after having asked the said William White what the paper was and being answered by him that it was his will.
>
> And that all of them the said John Hounslow, Mary Bristow and Thomas Badcock subscribed the said paper writing at different times.

And that they or any or either of them did not sign their his or her names or name thereto in the presence of the others or other of them

In their Answers the defendants come up with all sorts of other reasons why the Museum should not benefit. George White claimed that if the will was shown to be valid, then the British Museum could not claim all William White's estate as it was bequeathed in his will because the Law states that the British Museum was only capable of taking, holding or enjoying goods and chattels, lands, tenements, and hereditaments to the value of £500 per annum. George White claimed that the estate of William White greatly exceeded this amount, and that anyway in the year of William's death, the British Museum held goods or chattels equal to the full £500.

In addition to the dispute with the British Museum, there is also a question mark over William White's property in Hampshire. In his will he leaves 'My estate at Wildern in Hampshire my houses at Cowes and all other my real property I devise to me wife for life.' He leaves instructions in his will over Wildern:

I further direct that if I die without building on the said Estate at Wildern then my executors shall appropriate two thousand pounds of monies to be vested now in Exchequers Bills and lay out the same in building and improving the said estate, also it is my intention that ten thousand pounds now in the new four pounds per cent annuities shall be considered as part of the reversion of my property for it is in my power to dispose of it by will after the life interest of my said wife under the Settlement made on our marriage, my Uncle the said Henry Leigh and my mother best know my intentions and ideas of building at Wildern.

The defendants ask for the Court's direction regarding the Wildern estate:

But these Defendants believe that the said William White was in Equity entitled to a certain freehold estate called Wildern and Holmes near Southampton consisting of upwards of three hundred and forty four acres of arable meadow pasture and coppice lands with the timber thereon and a farm house barns and agricultural building two labourers cottages and gardens which he had agreed to purchase for the price or sum of seven thousand seven hundred pounds in part satisfaction of which he had paid the sum of seven hundred and seventy pounds but which purchase was not completed at the time of his death.

Like so many cases where there are disputes over wills, what must have seemed very straightforward when the will was written, becomes the subject of a lengthy and contentious argument in the courts. The Trustees of the British Museum were no doubt anxious to have their right to the property after the death of Caroline, William's wife, recognised. The fact that William's mother was still alive and that much of the property was in trust to her during her lifetime just added complications. The Wildern estate added yet another complication. The timeline relating to this case illustrates how much information is included in the case:

19 and 20 Dec 1798   Indentures of Settlement made between Catherine White then Catherine Leigh Spinster of the first part, John White Esquire of the second part, and Barnabus Leigh and George White Esquires of the third part: William White is entitled upon the death of his mother, Catherine White, to £5959 17s. 9d. 3 per cent consolidated bank annuities and £2,000 East India Stock.

15 Jan 1799 Will of John White.

25 Jan 1821   Indenture or Declaration of Trust made between William White of the one part and Catherine White of the other part: William White is up to the time of his death interested in

remainder or reversion expectant on the death or marriage of the said Catherine White to £20,000 bank consolidated 3 per cent annuities which were standing in the names of the said William White and Catherine White upon trust to permit the said Catherine White receive the dividends thereof during her life.

26 Jun 1821   Agreement made by the said Testator William White for the purchase of the said estate called Wildern and Holmes (also referred to as Wildern).

31 Dec 1821   Indenture of Settlement regarding the marriage of the said William White and Caroline Avis White (then Caroline Avis Bull) between William White of the first part, John Bull of the second part, Caroline Avis Bull now Caroline Avis White of the third part, and the Revd John Bull, Henry Bull and Richard Finch of the fourth: £10,000 Navy 5 pounds per cent annuities now converted into £10,500 new 4 per cent annuities are held by certain Trustees for William White and Caroline Avis White for their lives, whoever survives, and to be transferred to any child of theirs who reaches 21.

Dec 1821   Marriage of William White and Caroline Avis White.

10 Dec 1822   Will of William White: He leaves all real estate to his wife Caroline Avis White if she remains unmarried, then to his son, then to the heirs (male then female) of his son via the trust of Henry Leigh and John Bull, and then for Henry Leigh and John Bull to sell and give to the Trustees of the British Museum.

20 Mar 1823   Codicil of William White: After his wife's death all of his residuary property, instead of immediately going to the British Museum, will go via a trust for the use of his son. Also he says that after his death his wife must live wholly with his mother.

13 May 1823   Death of William White (the Testator).

30 May 1823   Henry Leigh and John Bull prove William White's Will.

9 July 1823   Indenture of Settlement between Henry Leigh and John Bull of the one part and Catherine White of the other part: Catherine White transferred the £20,000 bank consolidated 3 per cent annuities from the joint account of William White deceased and Catherine White into the joint names of Henry Leigh, John Bull and Catherine White. This is according to Indenture dated 25 January 1821 and allows Catherine White to receive the interest or dividends thereof in satisfaction of the annuity of £600 bequeathed to her by the Will of John White.

Mar 1824   Death of William John White, infant son of William White (the Testator).

6 July 1824   Bill of Complaint.

18 Oct 1824   Answer of George White.

16 Dec 1824   Answer of Catherine White, Caroline Avis White, and John Leigh and Henry Bull.

22 Jan 1825   Bill of Complaint amended by order.

PROBATE DISPUTE IN THE COURT OF REQUESTS
At a much simpler level, a dispute was brought to the Court of Requests in 1594 by Thomas Bushell on behalf of his children: Henry, Corbett, Mary, Ursula and Barbara. Anne Pople, who died five years before the case was brought, bequeathed each of the children a few pounds. Her executors have not paid the legacies, and there was apparently an agreement that two of the executors would hand over

Anne Pople's estate to the third executor. This third executor has now died and his wife has his estate, and is refusing to pay the children their small legacies. This case was brought to the Court of Requests as the amounts in question are small: £3 to Ursula, Barbara and Corbett, £5 to Henry and £10 to the daughter Mary.

ANOTHER PROBATE DISPUTE

Another case where the dispute is centred around a will is that of the Blossett Eyre family.[3] This Chancery case dates from 1818 and incorporates a variety of documents:

- Bill of Complaint.
- Answer.
- Supplemental Bill of Complaint.
- Three Interrogatories.
- Answers and examinations.

This case concerns the estate of the deceased Elizabeth Theodosia Eyre who in her will left the majority of her money to Theodosia Eyre Blosset, daughter of Major John Blosset who was serving in the 5th West India Regiment. This is to be paid as an allowance from stock dividends for her education until she turns 21 or marries. However John Blosset (on his daughter's behalf) accuses the executors of Elizabeth Theodosia Eyre's will, John Baker and John Morgan, of refusing to pay any such allowance.

In the initial bill it is stated that in Elizabeth Theodosia Eyre's will, dated 11 August 1816, she bequeathed the remainder of her money, securities for money, goods, chattels and personal estate and effects (after her other legacies, debts and testamentary expenses have been paid) to Theodosia Eyre Blosset. This fortune was to be converted into stocks (except the silver plate) and the dividends and profits from this to be used for Theodosia Eyre Blosset's education until she turned 21 or married. The silver plate was to be delivered to Theodosia Eyre Blosset immediately. The defendants John Baker and John Morgan were the executors of Elizabeth Theodosia Eyre's will.

Elizabeth Theodosia Eyre died on 9 October 1817 without having changed her will. The executors received Elizabeth Theodosia Eyre's personal estate and effects to 'a very considerable amount and much more than sufficient to pay and satisfy all her just debts and funeral and testamentary expenses'. However, the executors had not paid any form of allowance to John Blosset for his daughter Theodosia Eyre Blosset's education and maintenance, despite being requested several times. The executors have sometimes said that they refused because Major John Blosset's fortune was sufficient to maintain and educate his daughter. John Blosset refuted this and asked for an account of the Testatrix's personal estate upon and since her death.

The defendants in their Answer replied that they admitted that they were the executors of Elizabeth Theodosia Eyre's will and that they have since proved the will and come into possession of her estate. They admitted that John Blosset's solicitor Thomas Turner had once requested an allowance for Theodosia Eyre Blosset from the Testatrix's estate, but that this was the only such request they have received. 'They admit that they have refused to comply with such application having been advised that they ought not to do so without the direction of this Honourable Court.'

They included a Schedule of the Testatrix's estate and John Baker pointed out he was now 'in advance in account of the said Testatrix's estate in the sum of one hundred and forty one pounds and upwards for monies out of pocket.'

They agreed that the silver plate (referred to in the will) and the wearing apparel of Elizabeth Theodosia Eyre was in the custody of the executor John Morgan, who said that he will now dispose of it as the court wishes. They also point out that the estate was owed £100 by the Testatrix's brother-in-law Robert Eyre, and pointed out that although the estate was also possessed of consolidated annuities to the value of £1,550 and £1,598 19s., the latter was to pay a yearly annuity to Jemima Wilmott of £5.

In 1819 a supplemental bill was introduced as Theodosia Eyre Blosset seemed to be trying to make her brothers and sisters, Eliza Blosset, Thomas Eyre Blosset, John Blosset and Julia Blosset, defendants to her earlier Bill. The case was further heard before the Master of the Rolls on 1 December 1818, who decreed that a full account of the Testatrix's personal residue estate should be taken. In fact this supplementary case is merely a repetition of the previous case, although now including the plaintiff's brothers and sisters as defendants. There appears to be no sense of accusation against these brothers and sisters in this Bill. In their Answer they all agree with their sister the plaintiff.

The Interrogatories that are to be put to witnesses basically ask:

- Have the examinants received any money from the Testatrix's estate that was neither bequeathed to them nor their due? Have you sold anything and for how much?
- What money from the estate has been spent and why?
- Are there any debts outstanding?

Being a Chancery case of course this is very much more wordy:

First Interrogatory:
Have not your or some and what person or persons and who by name by your order or for your use or with your knowledge privity or consent possessed deceived or got in divers or some and what part or parts of the personal estate and effects of Elizabeth Theodosia Eyre deceased the Testatrix in the pleadings in this cause named not specifically bequeathed.

Did not such personal estates or some and what part or parts thereof consist of a leasehold estate or leasehold estates money in the public stocks or funds money or bonds and mortgages and notes of hand and bills of exchange or on any other and what security or securities arrears of rent due to the testatrix in her life time or rents accrued due since her decease in respect of such leasehold estate or leasehold estates household goods and furniture or ready money or some and which of such several matters and things and what other matter and things matters or things did such personal estate

147

and every part thereof consist of and what was the true and utmost values of each and every particular of such matter and things and personal estate.

Have not you or some and what person or persons and whom by your order or for your use or with your knowledge privity or consent sold or disposed of some and what part or parts of such personal estate and effects and for what price or prices sum or sums of money and was or were such personal estate and effects and ever or any and what part and parts thereof sold and disposed of for the full and utmost value thereof respectively, and what part or parts of such personal estate now remain unreceived and indisposed of and in whose hands custody or power in or are the same respectively, and what doth the same and every part thereof consist of an how and in what names is the same and every part thereof seemed.

Set forth the particulars of all and every the matter in this interrogatory enquired after and the natures kinds quantities qualities and true and utmost values of each particular and when and where and how and in what manner by whom and to whom for what and upon what account all and every such particular have been possessed received supplied and disposed of according to the best and utmost of your knowledge remembrance information and belief.

Second Interrogatory:
Have you or any and what person or persons and when by name on your account paid disbursed expended and allowed any and what sum or sums of money in or towards payment of the funeral expenses debts or legacies of the said testatrix Elizabeth Theodosia Eyre or otherwise on account of the said testatrix.

Set forth in full true and particular account of all and every sum and sums of money which have been so paid disbursed expended or allowed together with the times when the names of the persons to whom and the purposes for which the same have been so paid disbursed expended or allowed and whether all and every or any and which of such sums of money which have been so paid disbursed expended or allowed were just fully and particularly according to the best and utmost of your knowledge remembrance information and belief.

Third Interrogatory:

Are or is there any part or parts of the personal estate and effects of the said testatrix Elizabeth Theodosia Eyre now outstanding or which have or hath not been possessed or received by you or by any person or persons by your order or for your use?

And why and for what reason have or hath the same been suffered to be and remain outstanding and unreceived and how and in what manner is the same outstanding personal estate and every part thereof seemed and from whom by name due and owing.

Set forth a full true and particular account of the matters in this interrogatory enquired after fully and particularly according to the best and utmost of your knowledge remembrance information and belief.

The replies are given by the defendants on 1 December 1818, as examinants to the Interrogatories. In addition to the financial proceeds of the investments they show that they have paid the following people:

James Turner, baker
William Palmer, milkman
Ann Hemming, poulterer
Stephen Organ, grocer
Jane Edwards, washerwoman
Bally and Bartram, upholsterers
Margaret Davis, for wages

Margaret Bunsden, for wages
Elizabeth Hitchin, chairwoman
Emery and Co., wine merchants
E. Offer, mantua maker
William Osborne, butcher
Lucy Gibbons, chandler
James Collett, shoemaker
Meyler and Co., printers
Marmaduke Aston, for rent
Thomas Hughes, for disbursements
Harriet Walker, quit rent
Thomas Stillman, quit rent and land tax
John Langley, solicitor
Mary Fournier, schoolmistress
John Morgan, surgeon
William Back
Jemima Willmott, annuity
Samuel and John Baker, solicitors

This list again confirms how useful the records of the courts of equity can be in highlighting the way of life of the people involved, and it can help to bring them alive in a way that records even as detailed as a will or inventory cannot do.

There is also a nice touch in that Elizabeth Theodosia Eyre's clothes have not been sold as the defendants felt they were worth more to Theodosia Eyre Blosset as clothes than as the £15 they were thought to be worth.

MARRIAGE SETTLEMENT AND ANNUITY

This case revolves around the marriage settlement of Mary Hoskins and William Gifford by which, after the death of her husband, Mary should receive an annuity of £380. She was also to keep all the household goods which had been hers at the time of her marriage. Lands were put in trust to ensure that she would receive her £380 annuity, however Benjamin Gifford, her father-in-law managed to take possession of all of his son's property, supposedly to secure his grandson's inheritance after Mary's death.[4]

This case gives us a real insight into the character of Benjamin Gifford.[5]

In 1694 Mary Gifford of Horsington in Somerset and her children brought a case to the Court of Chancery against her father-in-law Benjamin Gifford, following the death of her husband William Gifford. This should have been a very simple case and scarcely worthy of comment, however, mainly because of the intransigence of the defendant Benjamin Gifford, it dragged on for many years. There is only a small cast of principal characters: Mary Gifford (good), her children (good), Benjamin Gifford her father-in-law (bad) and trustees (insignificant as overruled by Benjamin).

Ten years earlier, in 1684, Mary Hoskins was set to marry William Gifford, and being an heiress great care was taken by her father to ensure that her interests were well looked after.

William Gifford's family lands were in Warminster, Horton, Bishopstrow and Boreham in Wiltshire, and in Cucklington, Horsington and Cheriton in Somerset. Mary came from Beaminster in Dorset and the manors of Beaminster Prima and Beaminster Seconda were held in trust for her. After their eventual marriage William and Mary end up living in Horsington, which is midway between their two ancestral homes.

The terms of the marriage settlement were fairly standard and should not have given rise to any dispute in the event of William Gifford dying before his wife Mary:

- Mary would pay £3,500 to William as her marriage portion.
- William would grant an annuity of £380 to Mary in the event of his death to be secured on some of William's lands.
- The lands charged with the annuity were to descend in tail male, subject to a further charge of £4,000 for the daughters' portions.
- Mary was to retain the profits of all her own lands for her own use.

- Mary was to have £3,500 for her own use.
- Mary was to keep all household goods which had been hers at the time of the marriage.

This fairly straightforward marriage agreement should have been sufficient, but the Hoskins family must have had severe doubts over the honesty and integrity of the Gifford family, and it took two agreements and three bonds to be absolutely sure that Mary would not suffer in the event of William's death, with trustees firmly in place.

1685 Jan	Marriage settlement.
1685 Jan	Agreement to levy a fine and to provide for younger children.
1685	Bond by William Gifford to the trustees for £2,000 to secure the terms of the settlement.
1685 Dec	Deed from William Gifford to trustees confirming that Mary would retain the right to her own copyhold lands and all her own lands and money over and above the £3,500 marriage portion which was paid to William. She was also to have all the household goods that she brought to the marriage which were valued at £441 4s. 10d.
1685 Dec	Bond by William Gifford to the trustees for £2,000 to pay Mary £1,000 on death of William.

The amount of paperwork to cover this fairly simple marriage contract, suggests that Mary's family were already a little suspicious of the Gifford family.

Benjamin and William Gifford also made assurances that the lands charged with the annuity were free from any encumbrance, although acknowledgement was made that by Benjamin's own marriage settlement of 1656 he had only a life interest, however the lands were then to descend to his eldest son, who was William, so this should not have given rise to any query.

The marriage duly took place and one hopes that William and Mary were happy for the few years that they had together. They had the following children:

Benjamin
Alice
Mary
Benjamin, after the death of the first one
John Hoskins
Dorothy

All is well until Benjamin is short of money and decides to transfer a mortgage he holds of a farm called Smallbrook in Warminster to his son William. This means that William will have paid him the £1,000 value of the mortgage, and will await his own repayment from the original mortgagor. This later becomes one of the main subjects of dispute in the case as Benjamin denies transferring the mortgage to William or receiving the £1,000.

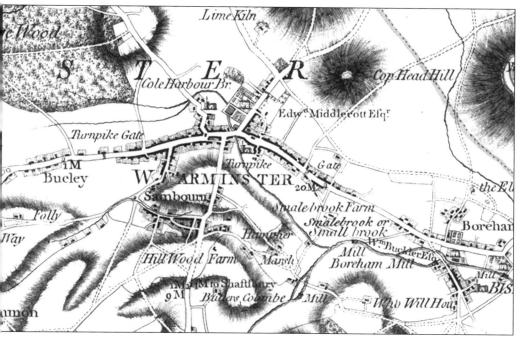

A map of Smallbrook Farm.

William Gifford, who from the little we hear of him, seems to have been a good man, and it is to be hoped that his marriage to Mary was a love match, perhaps with a little reservation on her father's part which led to the overkill on documents to secure her future in the event of William's premature death. William realised that no proper and secure provision had been made for his younger children and so bought Exchequer annuities for £800 which would give each of them £28 a year income.

In 1690 William made some notes for a will, and left these with his father who 'wrested' them from him. William decided to go and visit his father and get the papers back. He does so, and then stops off at Mrs Holiday's house on the way back and leaves the papers there by mistake. Mrs Holiday, perhaps trying to be helpful or perhaps in the pay of Benjamin, takes them back to Benjamin. William assumes that they are lost for ever.

We next see William very sick in bed and dictating the terms of his will. He has had more children than were mentioned in the notes that he had left in Mrs Holiday's house, which he believes anyway to be lost, so as far as William is concerned, this is his will. There is nothing strange about the terms of this will. He appoints his wife Mary, his father Benjamin Gifford and his father-in-law John Hoskins as executors. Mary is to have all the goods at the Beaminster estate, and all his goods and furniture in the house in Horsington except the items which he had been given by his father. He confirms the annuities of £28 on each of his younger children, from the Exchequer annuities. The executors are asked to fund the education and maintenance of the younger children as they think proper. This all seems straightforward, and no doubt would have been if William had not had a fit and died on 26 September 1693 before the will was properly signed and witnessed.

We now reach the stage where William has died, Mary is left a widow with five young children. She tells Benjamin, her father-in-law, of William's death and lets him know that she has this will which she intends to prove, even though it has not been signed.

We now start to see Benjamin in his true colours. He immediately

154

strings together the papers from the original notes for the 1690 will, the ones that William believed were lost in Mrs Holiday's house, and rushes off to have these proved as the proper will of William. This duly goes ahead and he is recognised as the sole executor of the estate. This will makes no mention of course of the children who were born after the notes were made, and also makes no mention of Mary. Presumably William thought she was well covered by what appeared to be very secure terms of the marriage contract.

Mary brings a Bill of Complaint to the Court of Chancery and tells us that Benjamin has taken over all William's lands and possessions including those that she brought to the marriage which were supposed to be hers for ever; he has sold many of William's cows and other goods to the value of £7,000. He has completely failed to pay her the £380 annuity and he is threatening to make her pay for the children's upkeep out of her own money. He is also claiming that she owes him £1,000 for a loan that he made to William. The marriage settlement has been completely disregarded and the trustees have failed to protect Mary's interests. On top of all this Benjamin has managed to get all the deeds and documents that might support her case into his own keeping, including the mortgage of Smallbrook Farm and the paperwork for the Exchequer annuities. Benjamin keeps up a string of threats against Mary saying that she will see 'black and blue days', that her marriage settlement is invalid and that he will force her to release her jointure or else he will 'perfectly ruin and beggar' her and her children.

Having had this rather dark picture of Benjamin drawn by Mary, we now turn to Benjamin's Answer in hopes that he can re-establish his reputation. He starts by denying all knowledge of the detail of the marriage settlement, saying that Mary has it in her custody. He also denies any knowledge of either the bond for £2,000 by the trustees concerning Mary's interest in the Beaminster manors or the bond for £1,000 which is to be paid to Mary on the death of William. He says that he would never have agreed to the latter had he known about it as Mary already had very generous jointure. This leads us to wonder whether Mary's father suggested it and that it was in fact done without Benjamin's knowledge as extra security for Mary's future. With such careful provision for Mary's security, was there some fear that William was not very healthy and might not live long, or was Mary's father just very wary of her scheming father-in-law?

Benjamin denies all knowledge of the mortgage that was transferred or any loan that might have been made to him by William. He also of course denies all knowledge of the will dictated by William just before his death.

He agrees that William bought the Exchequer annuities for £800 which were to pay out £28 per annum during the lives of the children, but he claims that William borrowed £1,000 from him to do this. He denies that the annuities were in trust for the children.

Chancery records are full of feuds between family members, but the callous behaviour of Benjamin to do down his own grandchildren is astonishing even by Chancery standards.

In his defence Benjamin claims that the will that he proved, made up from the notes that William thought were lost, appoints him as one of the executors and guardians of William and Mary's son Benjamin. Mary pointed out this Benjamin died and the surviving son Benjamin was born after this supposed will was written, however Benjamin senior disputed this saying that the only children born after the death of William were John Hoskins Gifford and Dorothy.

In a complete reversion of the marriage settlement he tries to conciliate Mary by offering her back the £3,500 that she brought to the marriage in return for a discharge from all other liabilities.

Benjamin always claims that he is acting out of the best interests of the eldest grandson Benjamin and that he believes that Mary has plenty of money to provide for the two youngest children, John Hoskins Gifford and Dorothy, who were born after the will was made. He even goes so far as to say that he and William had many discussions about these younger children and William agreed that Mary had a very good jointure and could support these children herself. He then goes on to say that the reason that Mary has not received her annuity of £380 is that she hasn't asked for it. So many statements in the courts of equity can only evoke the response 'Really??!!'.

Benjamin obviously had quite a strong hold over William for when discussing the alleged will which was left at Mrs Holiday's house, he claims that he wrote and told William that it was not lost and that he had it back again. William then, apparently, said that his wife must know nothing of this will 'for if she had he the said William should have no peace'. Perhaps William was in thrall to both his wife and his father and told each a different story in hopes of keeping the peace, little envisaging the havoc that would ensue in court when Mary tried to get control of what she believed was due to her.

Benjamin also states that he should not make any claim on the estate, such as paying Mary the £1,000 owed to her on the bond, until the eldest son Benjamin was aged 21.

There is also a joint Answer given by the other defendants: Arthur Symes, Edward Middlecott, Henry Whatman, Richard Bayley and John Foster. This is rather refreshing as they are slightly more independent and perhaps truthful.

They seem to agree with Benjamin that the will that he proved was the valid one, however Symes does confirm Mary's story of William's deathbed instructions for his will.

A nice detail is added over the payment of the £3,500 jointure at the time of the marriage. At the time Mary asked whether it should be brought into the room where they were, but Benjamin replied that it would be all right if it was paid straight to William, who then signed a receipt for it dated 5 November 1685. They later say that a computation showed that actually more than the £3,500 had been paid.

They report that William used to complain that his father was still receiving all the rents from the lands in the marriage agreement. He suggested to Mary that they move from Beaminster where they were living, but felt that even if they were in Wiltshire they would not get much in the way of rents.

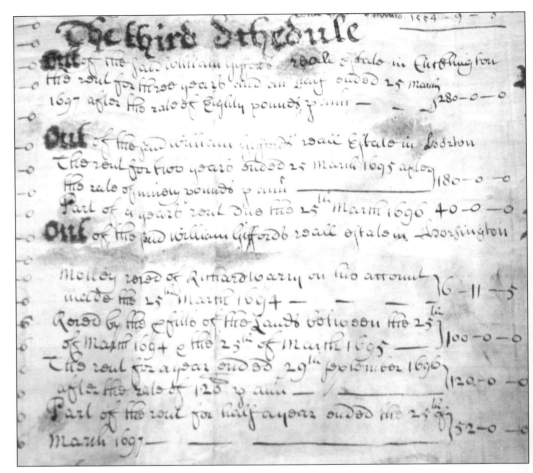

Schedule of rents from Chancery Depositions, C 22/976/9.

They also confirm that Benjamin knew perfectly well that the Exchequer annuities were intended to be for the benefit of the younger children.

Symes then gives some nice detail about the days immediately following William's death concerning the will that Benjamin later proved:

> He rode to the defendant Benjamin's house and told him what had happened whereupon the said Benjamin acquainted the defendant that the testator had about two or three years

since before that made his will which the said Benjamin said he had not then the same, but was informed the said testator had sometime left it with some friends and he would look after it and when found show it to the defendant, and shortly after, by the complainant Mary the mother's order, he the defendant having received notice that the defendant Benjamin desired to speak with him went to his house and told him promising there had been no such will as pretended, the defendant Benjamin having as he conceived made such an uncertain relation of it that in case the defendant Benjamin would admit the said complainant Mary the mother to administer she would limit a trust to him and others that might be the nearest to the intention of the will, but to have a share of the government of children herself and she designed no benefit thereby, to which the said defendant Benjamin said he had ordered his cousin to ask her if she would renounce the administration if she would then she might then have said so, but it was then too late.

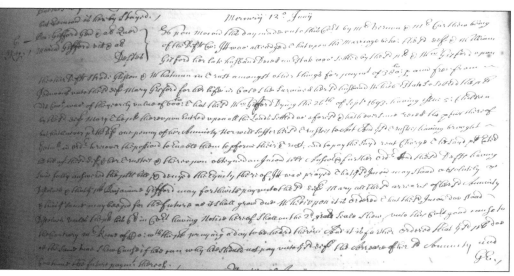

An Order relating to the Gifford case, C 33/283.

Symes gives us an excellent vision of Benjamin whom he describes as a 'melancholy man'. He is certain that he 'suspects the said Benjamin had much imposed on the said William his son for that the said defendant Benjamin had got the mortgages from Bennet into this hands'. We also hear that Benjamin intended to threaten Mary into renouncing her annuity by exclaiming to Symes that he 'would marry a young wife and raise a new family and first ruin the infants and then the mother'. What a vindictive man!

MANAGING PROPERTY FROM AFAR

Have a thought for William Maltin, a yeoman of the parish of Lyndridge, Worcestershire, and his wife Bridget who inherited a cottage in the township of Aston Co. Montgomery, valued at 20s. per year, some 30 miles from where they lived.

Thomas Brown claimed that he and his wife Joyce agreed to buy it from William Maltin for £5. As a Richard Hicks was living in the cottage, they got an order ejectment against him which they paid for. When Thomas Brown came to hand over the £5 to William Maltin, he was refused. It transpired that Thomas Mason, who was the solicitor for Richard Hicks, had offered William Maltin £6 for the cottage, boasting 'how cheap a bargain this was'. Thomas Brown brings the case to the Court of Chancery claiming that:

> having no habitation for himself wife and four children and being a very poor man and being desirous to have a poor habitation for himself and wife in the their old age not being able to work for their livelihood did sell and dispose of his goods and chattels and thereby did raise money to bear and defray the charges of the said suit and for the obtaining and the possession of the premises and did satisfy the same.

We can but imagine him with no goods and no property expecting to move into the cottage, and being frustrated. He further gains our sympathy with the phrase: 'so your distressed orator might not in his old age be exposed to the world without house or harbour'.

When William Maltin puts in his Answer, we realise that there is a bit more to it. The cottage actually belongs to William's wife Bridget who inherited it from her father. As the cottage was 'in a distant county and unknown to them', they accepted the help of Thomas Brown who pretended he had 'great powers and interest in the said county and acquaintance with many practitioners of the law in these parts' to obtain an order of ejectment for the tenant Richard Hicks. William Maltin said that he never agreed to sell the cottage to Thomas Brown. Growing suspicious of Thomas Brown, William and Bridget Maltin travelled to the cottage and there discovered that the then tenant Isaac Howell was paying the rent to Thomas Brown, who then refused entry to them, despite no sale having taken place.

William and Bridget then agreed with Thomas Mason (Richard Hicks's lawyer) that they would sell him the cottage at a price of £6 to them, with an additional payment of £4 to Richard Hicks to put a stop to any future lawsuit. There was an indenture to this effect dated 25 June 1678. Thomas Mason does not have good things to say about Thomas Brown:

> he hath had a very ill fame of the Complainant [Thomas Brown] to be a very bad neighbour and the said cottage standing near this defendant's [Thomas Mason] estate and the said plaintiff if he should continue as bad as he is reported might have been very prejudicial unto this defendant in his sheep and cattle.

The moral seems to be that you should not try to manage property from a distance, and that you cannot know who to trust if you have to do this.

MERCHANTS AND MARINERS

A case in 1707 was brought by Benjamin Braine a merchant of London.[6] He was the owner of a ship, the *Mayflower*, which set off on a voyage to Virginia. The crew persuaded John Ellis, the ship's master, to sail to Carlisle Bay, Barbados, West Indies, where he died.

The mate then took possession of the master's papers and the ship was declared unfit and sold. The dispute brought to court was concerned with the payment of wages and the loss of the ship which Braine thought had not been unfit and should not have been sold. The defendants in the case are named as William Cavett, mariner and mate, Timothy Cookney, Elizabeth Hook, widow, John Cornelius (alias John Cornelis), mariner, Daniel Campanell, mariner, Joseph Bradley, mariner, John Belt, mariner, John Baton, mariner, Benjamin Lewis, mariner, William Lewis, mariner, Edward Essex, mariner, Ogel Pearce, mariner, John Martin, mariner, and Thomas Ellis, mariner. This case is typical of a great number brought to court and although there is not very much genealogical information, there is an insight into the life of the characters involved and of course a historian of trade with the West Indies or Virginia would find this sort of case of value.

TRADES AND TRADESMEN

In 1585 John Malmoye, a citizen and fruiterer of London, went into partnership with his near kinsman Richard Roothe. This went well for a bit until they came to do their accounts, and Richard Roothe decided to end the partnership. They agreed that John Malmoye would take over the many debts and credits and the goods of the trade, and pay Richard Roothe £80. Malmoye then paid Roothe the first £30 and agreed to a bond for the remaining £50, which Roothe kept in his custody. Malmoye then paid another £20, leaving £30 outstanding, however this was mostly offset by the £26 that was owed by Roothe's wife for goods that were delivered to her house, particularly when Roothe was away in Ireland. Notwithstanding this, Richard Roothe 'being covetously bent and minding to convey himself to Ireland has most ungodlyly procured your poor suppliant to be arrested upon the said bill of £50'. There follow Answers by Richard Roothe and Alexander Roothe, Interrogatories and Depositions and, rather more interesting, the accounts of the money paid by Malmoye to Roothe have been attached as part of the case. Account of money and wares delivered by John Malmoy, citizen and fruiterer of London:

To wife of Richard Rothe when he lay sick in April 1585	£10
For fruits delivered to Richard from 24th January 1585 to 6th March 1585	£14 12s. 8d.
Delivered to wife of Richard Roth as much fruit from 12 June 1585 to 28th January next	£3 3s. 6d.
Delivered to his wife from time to time from 20 August 1585 to 30 September next	50s.
Lent to Richard Rothe at the Castle in Paternoster Row	20s.
Paid Richard Harris	£4 5s.
That he does owe John Malmoy	14s.
Richard Roth received at Mr Cornewell for chives and pears	£3 11s.
Paid a Dutchman for Richard Roth	£3
He was to answer for 2¹/₂ loads of coal	20s.
Lent him the town Malling for faggots	£3 18s.
He owes to me upon a reckoning at Newcastle	43s.

A search of the online catalogue shows that fruiterers and many other citizens and tradesmen in London brought cases to the courts of equity, which will all, no doubt, add significantly to the history of London.

Useful information on the history of trades can be gleaned from these records, such as the case defended by William Cooper of Glastonbury in 1638, a worsted maker with several servants and apprentices, for which we only have the Answer.[7]

William Cooper denies that he agreed to pay 20 marks to build an outworking house in the tenement for his own trade of worstedmaking with the plaintiff finding the timber, as is claimed by the plaintiff. Rather, William lent the plaintiff the money to do this. At the end of the seven years it was agreed that the plaintiff would repay William Cooper the money and would leave the premises. There is rather more to this as the plaintiff has come to the defendant as an adult apprentice and the case shines a light on the difficulty of keeping an apprentice:

In June 1637 the plaintiff, being then 28 years of age came to the defendant and told the defendant he was greatly in debt and in much want and did not know what course to take to maintain himself, his wife and child and asked the defendant, William Cooper, to teach him the trade of worsted comber for which he would pay him £10.

Hoping that the plaintiff would become comfortable as the rest of the defendant's servants were, he agreed to teach him for £10. He taught him so well that within six months the plaintiff was able to earn as much money each week as a journeyman. The plaintiff then grew disorderly and when the defendant (keeping 400 poor people at work) should depend upon his labour the plaintiff would not only refuse to work but also endeavour to hinder the defendant's other servants from their ancient and accustomed use of working with the defendant. The plaintiff then peremptorily and without any warning departed from the defendant's work to the great loss and hindrance of the defendant. As with so many cases brought to court, one's faith in humanity is rather shaken. The plaintiff in this case seems to be a most unpleasant character – which might be rather unwelcome news if he was your ancestor.

AMERICAN CONNECTION

Many cases in the courts of equity concern people in America, and can be useful in pinpointing the English place of origin for an emigrant, with some certainty that the family really is the right one. A case in 1706 concerns the estate of Cope Doyly, late rector of Williamsburgh who died in Virginia where he lived, possessed of goods and lands, in particular an estate with slaves (negro, mulatto and white), tobacco, cattle, etc. worth about £2,500.[8] Doyly had dealings with merchants on both sides of the Atlantic, including the defendants who were merchants in London. He was a widower who died intestate leaving two young orphaned children, aged 12 and 6. The plaintiff, his brother, Robert Doyly, rector of Margaret Roding in the County of Essex in England, was the administrator of his

164

estate and the crux of the argument was over the estate in Virginia. Robert Doyly accused Cope's partners, Micajah Perry, Robert Perry and Thomas Lane who were all merchants in London, of taking possession of Cope Doyly's estate and acting irresponsibly with it. After assuring Robert Doyly that the estate would be secure and safe for Cope's two sons, and that they would improve it for their benefit, these partners have instead taken the proceeds for themselves and have irresponsibly lent money from it to Benjamin Harrison, another defendant, who lived in Virginia, and who is known to be unreliable and not good at repaying his debts. Robert Doyly accused the partners of collusion and confederacy, and says that they have refused to work with him in the administration of the estate, having failed to provide any of the necessary deeds, documents, etc. The record of the courts of equity can sometimes use quite emotive language, giving a clue as to the character of the people involved. In this case we find these words in the Bill:

> Whereas at the time of any such payment or answering the said Harrison was a person of very small or no reputation as to the fairness of his dealings or his substance, responsibleness or ability to answer what hath been to him so paid.

This receives a taunting reply in the Answer:

> do look upon the said Harrison both for Integrity and Sufficiency in Estate to be at least equal to the complainant.

That is to say, if the complainant says Harrison lacks integrity, then he is equal to him.

Useful dates can be inferred in this case:

> Cope Doyly, a widower left Charles Doyly his eldest son and heir at law and Cope Doyly his second son and his only children then living and both of them infants of tender years and much under their respective ages of one and twenty years,

that is to say Charles of the Age Twelve years or thereabouts and the Cope of the age of six years or thereabouts.

The defendants Micajah Perry, Thomas Lane and Richard Perry in their Answer deny any wrongdoing, and of using money for themselves. They had been assured by the court in Virginia that Benjamin Harrison was the children's guardian there, and so had released money to him for their care. The Order from Virginia said that Charles Doyly being over the age of 14 on 2 June 1704 was able to choose his own guardian, and had chosen Harrison. Unlike the plaintiff, the defendants believe that Harrison is reliable. They annexed accounts for the estate with their answer and asked for a guarantee that this should protect them from any further applications by Robert Doyly or Charles Doyly in the future.

FIELD NAMES

The courts of equity are a mine of information for local history. They can name fields and plots of land such as in an involved case about lands in the parish of Studland in Dorset of 1671:[9]

a certain mead called South Meadow a close called the East Grow and Sandy Hills with the combe thereto belonging,
a close called the Deane Close,
lands called the Furze Field,
a meadow called Olwell Meadow,
lands or moor called the Moors,
and certain closes called Rycrofts,
and twelve acres of arable called the Lyons,
certain parcels of land called Shortland,
fields and common of pasture for 220 sheep and for other beasts or horses to pasture on the downs commons and waste grounds of Godlingston

In a case of 1722 the plaintiff Philip Nicholas of Bristol claimed that his great grandfather was seised in 1650 of the following lands:[10]

all that messuage or tenement one oxhouse thereunto adjoining one orchard one meadow containing by estimation four acres or thereabouts five parcels of land arable pastoral and wood containing by estimation thirty acres (be it more or less) situate lying and being in the parish of Newchurch in the said county of Monmouth and purchased by the said Phillip Nicholas of Merrick Howell als Hooper.

And also one other messuage or tenement on parcel of meadow containing three acres or thereabouts and one close of ground containing four acres or thereabouts lying in Newchurch aforesaid and which the said Phillip Nicholas purchased of James David als Hopper nearing and abutting on the west and north sides to a lane leading from a place called Pullegwyllin towards the Abbey of Tynterne and on the east side to the waste grounds or common adjoining to Chepstow Park and on the south part to one close called Kae maine then in the tenure of Charles John Steven and nearing and abutting on the south west side to a close then called Kae maine in the tenure of the said Charles John Steven and lying in the parish of Kilgurring.

FORMER MONASTIC LANDS

A case brought to the Court of the Star Chamber in the reign of Edward VI (1547–53) shines a light on the difficulties of establishing the ownership of manorial lands after the Dissolution of the Monasteries, and the rights to common land.[11] The dispute centres on the manor of Roundhill in Somerset, and was brought by John White, Richard Brethren, John Barbour, Stephen Gane, Nicholas Bretyn, John Leg, John Parker, John Moggs, John Marshe, John Grene, who were all tenants of Sir William Stourton Lord Stourton of the manor of Roundhill.

The tenants hold several divers messuages lands of Lord Stourton's manor of Roundhill for terms of lives and terms of years and have always had use of the wastes and commons, common of pasture for alimentation of beasts and cattle to come at all times in the year at their will and pleasure, and also to have fuel to spend in their houses and tenements growing in and upon the same wastes and commons and also timber for the reparation and building of their said tenements likewise growing in and upon the said wastes together with cart bote plough bote and hedge bote. However on 20th July 1546 Richard Zouche Esq of a malicious mind that he bears as well against the plaintiffs as against Lord Stourton has wrongfully enclosed and caused to be enclosed part of the waste ground belonging to the said manor of Roundhill, by means whereof the complainants cannot have and take such common of pasture with their beasts or have use of the timber and fuel wood growing on the said wastes, which the plaintiffs and all other tenants of the said manor have always used to have as is said for the necessary reparation and building of their houses and for their fuel hedge bote plough bote and cart bote, and he has utterly excluded the complainants and all other tenants of the manor to their utter undoing.

Richard Zouche not contented with the injuries and misbehaviour, but minding nothing else but trouble and disquiet of your said poor subjects with new inventions and devises has of late, since the said enclosure, made, in a thicket of wood and in a desert place being parcel of waste ground in the said manor of Roundhill, a suspicious pound, where as there was at no time any made heretobefore, and often times the said Richard Zouche and his servants very prively and unknown to your subjects make privy drifts of your said poor subjects' beasts and cattle pasturing in and upon the said waste ground and driving them to the said suspicious pound being a place more like for thieves to hide themselves in than meet for a common pound.

Being a Star Chamber case, there has to be violence involved, so we next hear that:

Now the said John White one of your poor subjects being in and upon part of the waste ground of the said manor of Roundhill near the suspicious pound in God's peace, that is to say on 22nd May 1547 the said Robert Mauncell otherwise called Robert Rowff being a coming quarreler and oppressor of your poor subjects, having a great staff of length of 7 feet in his hands the said day of May then and there assaulted John White and with the said piked staff did beat him upon the head and other parts of his body and did grievously hurt and wound him in his left hand and prick him throughout his left hand with one of the pikes and maimed him and the said Robert not content but of his further malicious mind minding nothing else but to flay and kill John White did then and there with the said piked staff crush and break all the bones in his right arm and so departed leaving him dead, of which said assault beating wounding and hurt he is not only maimed in his right hand and arm and left hand and lost the usage thereof forever to his utter undoing, but also is and shall be the worse in his body and limbs all his days to his great pain and shortening of his life.

A very typical phrase in the equity courts then follows:

Richard Zouche is son and heir apparent to Lord Zouch and a man greatly friended allied and maintained in the county, your said poor subjects therefore being poor husbandmen cannot have any remedy against him and his servants in the said county. The tenants live in fear of murder or man slaughter and dare not bring a case against Richard Zouche.

Richard Zouche in his Answer claims that the land in question does not belong to Lord Stourton at all and therefore the tenants have no right to pasture their cattle on the waste ground nor to have any of the wood. He then gives a brief history of the land:

Henry VII was seised of the lands by right of his imperial crown of the site of the cell of Stavordell belonging to the late prior of Taunton and of all those lands meadows pastures commons feedings and hereditaments commonly called Meryhill Cornehold Cowyslease le Grove Broad Meade Priors Mead and Le Croft with the appurtenances in Staverdell parcel of the possessions of the late prior of Taunton, and of and in one wood called Priors Wood containing 120 acres in Staverdell parcel of the said late priory of Taunton which said wood which the complainants suppose to be waste belonging to a farm called Roundhill parcel of the said late cell, all which premises before the Dissolution of the said priory were occupied with the said late cell by the governors of the same for the time being by the appointment and at the will of the late priors of the late prior of Taunton and the said late King being seised of the said late cell and other the premises by his letters patent dated 29 April 1544 did give and grant the said late cell by the name of all that his capital messuage and farm of Staffordell with the appurtenances and all the singular other the premises to John now Earl of Oxford to have and to hold to him and his heirs for ever whereof the same Earl was of the premises seised in his demesne as of fee and so being seised by good and lawful covenant in the law did give and grant all the late cell by the name of all his said capital messuage in Staverdell and all the premises by the said letters patent granted to the said Earl unto the said Richard Zouche to have to him and to his heirs forever.

A large number of people are then called to give Depositions. Deponents for John White, Lord Stourton:

John Dyer of Wincanton, gent tenant to Lord Stourton and to Richard Zouche, age 50.
Henry Zethe of Stourton, servant and tenant to Lord Stourton, age 40.

John Matthewe of Horsington. husbandman, age 30.

Henry Spender of Horsington, age 40.

Philip Thomas of Barrow, husbandman, age 44.

Walter Moore of Penne, husbandman, age 40.

John Sparrowe of Penne, husbandman, age 40.

John Vyning of Wincanton, tenant to Lord Stourton, age 36.

William Mondaie of Wincanton, tenant to Lord Stourton, age 30.

William Jacob of Clopton in the parish of Cucklington, husbandman, age 50.

Robert Vyning of Wincanton, tenant to Lord Stourton, age 36.

Nicholas Keekes of Gillingham yeoman, tenant to Lord Stourton, age 40.

Deponents for Richard Zouche:

John Glynne of Wincanton yeoman, age 52, tenant of Richard Zouche.

Richard Kendall of Wincanton, husbandman tenant of Richard Zouche, age 80.

John Milward of Stony Stoke, tenant of Richard Zouche, age 50.

Henry Skoffer of Cucklington, husbandman tenant to Richard Zouche, age 70.

William Rede of Cucklington, husbandman tenant to the Earl of Arundel, age 70.

James Wylton of Cole in the parish of Bruton, husbandman, age 70.

Robert Hyllinge of Penn, husbandman, age 72.

John Butt of Penne, husbandman, age 40.

John Hyllinge of Penn, husbandman, age 60.

Robert Burporte of Marnhull, yeoman, age 45.

John Edwards of Stony Stoke, husbandman tenant to Richard Zouche, age 70.

They give evidence on the ownership of the land, particularly by showing to whom they paid rent. John Dyer of Wincanton says:

Depositions relating to Roundhill Manor, STAC 3/3/80.

He holds the messuage or grange called Roundhills farm demised to him by William late prior of Taunton for the term of his life and others, by indenture dated 10 August 26 Henry VIII [1534]. He paid all the fines heriots amerciaments of courts reliefs and estrays to the prior. He had sufficient hedge boot house boot plough boot fire boot and fold boot to be taken off and in the wood being in the forest of Selwood when and as often as there should be need in and upon the premises. The farmers of the said grange of Roundhill and the customary tenants of the barrow ought and have used to have common for rudder beasts and horse and pannage for swine at all times in the year within the wood called Priors wood and other the waste ground within the forest of Selwood.

He adds confusion to this by saying that the prior of Staverdell for the time being was parson of the parish of Wincanton 'which parish of Wincanton does extend to the borders of the said parcels of ground. A mill fast by the house of Staverdell does pay tithing to Wincanton but if any died within the house of Staverdell priory they were buried within the said priory'. He does not know if the site of the cell is within the parish of Wincanton.

Henry Zethe is quite clear that he holds the lands from Lord Stourton as lord of the manor of Roundhill:

> the farmer and tenants of Roundhill and Barrow have always used to have common of pasture for rudder beasts horses and swine at all times in the year within the waste and commons belonging to the said manor of Roundhill and he never heard of Roundhill being called anything other than a manor. Richard Zouche has enclosed a parcel of ground containing 4 acres of the waste and common where the farmers and tenants of Roundhill and Barrow ought to have common and pasture for their cattle. Richard Zouche has caused to be felled in Priors wood a great part of the timber there in the which wood the tenants of Roundhill and Barrow have used to have timber for the necessary reparations of their houses.

Will Rydhed agrees with him:

> He was servant in Roundhill to the prior of Stavordell for 10 years and bailiff of the grounds and cattle of Roundhill and Staverdell for 10 years, which Roundhill has always been called a manor and courts have been kept there yearly and the tenants of Barrow and Wincanton being several homages have come to the courts yearly.
>
> Being bailiff he has delivered timber to the tenants and the tenants have used to cut short brushed wood for their brewing and baking at a place in the forest against Holt Hill called the Tail which they have always had by licence of the bailiff.

The Depositions given on behalf of Richard Zouche paint a slightly different picture. John Glynne says that:

> He has known the site of the late cell of Staverdell sometime belonging to the late prior of Taunton and has known the same and the other parcel of land about 25 years. The same

173

cell and all the lands being the demesne pertaining to the said cell of Staverdell have not been belonging and annexed to the priory of Taunton above 10 years before the dissolution of the said priory of Taunton which before that time as he says was reputed and taken for a priory by itself of the foundation of Lord Zouche and his ancestors as he has heard said. Richard Zouche has been seised of the said site of the cell and other premises of an estate of inheritance for 2 years last past conveyed him by a purchase from Sir Thomas Arundel knight which was purchased of the King's majesty by the Earl of Oxford and by him granted to Sir Thomas Arundel. Within a distance of half a mile of the forest of Selwood lies a certain farm called the farm or grange of Roundhill pertaining to the said prior of Taunton. Richard Zouche is owner of an estate of inheritance of the wood called Prior's wood and says that the said wood is parcel of the lands belonging to the said cell by the like conveyance of the said cell and not appertaining to the said farm of Roundhill, and the farm of Roundhill has always been reputed as a farm pertaining to the cell of Staverdell.

A student of the dispersal of monastic lands after the Dissolution would find cases such as this essential reading.

STOPPING UP OF A FOOTPATH
Many examples of trespass are brought to the Court of the Star Chamber, such as one in 1613.[12] Robert White, a butcher who 'disliked the neighbourhood of Stephen Coles' and tried to make Coles 'weary of dwelling there' and to bar him from the way to the church and market, procured two or three great nasty dogs that would bite and pull down any that came that way. To add a little emphasis to White's treachery we are told that these dogs nearly killed Hugh Barbor and Robert Daws and divers others. Then Robert White 'not content with this outrageous and uncivil plot of keeping these biting dogs' but intended to stop up and bar the footway from

Stephen Coles's house and also the houses of eleven others 'for the fuller effecting of his devilish and wicked plot and practice did conspire with Hugh Kemys, John King, Richard Jacob, Henry Lane and John Dornford how to do this'. Not only was Stephen Coles prevented from walking along the footpath to get into town, but he was 'barred from the way to the church and market whereby your subject nor his family should have any way or means to hear God's word read or preached, nor should get any provision from the market for himself and his family'. As always with these cases, they tug on your heartstrings, as we imagine Stephen Cole and his family not daring to leave their house to get to church.

Chapter 6

CASE STUDY –
JANE AUSTEN CONNECTION

Cases brought to the courts of equity can be of interest to biographers. A quick search of the index reveals references to well-known authors, politicians, architects and members of the aristocracy, amongst others.

Jane Austen was of particular interest to one of my postgraduates who had studied English literature. On researching the catalogue, we identified the Lefroy v Lefroy case of 1825–32 as being potentially significant. What was not realised was just how involved this case would be, and the wealth of information that would emerge.

The case revolves around the will of Revd John Henry George

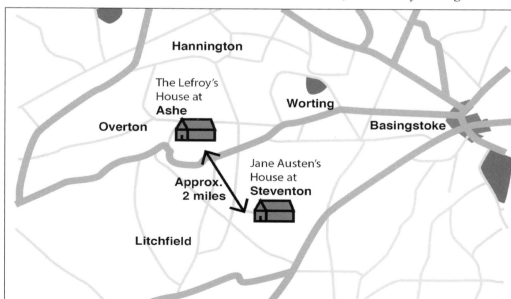

A plan showing the proximity of places to Jane Austen's house in the case of Lefroy v Lefroy.

Ashe Rectory House, where the Revd John Henry George Lefroy, the testator, grew up.

Lefroy, who died on 5 September 1823 and is referred to throughout the case as 'the testator'. Benjamin Lefroy, the testator's brother, was married to Jane Anna Elizabeth Austen, who was the daughter of Revd James Austen, who in turn was the brother of Jane Austen the author. Madam Ann Lefroy, the mother of the testator, was known to have been a great friend of the author's and was the aunt of Tom Langlois Lefroy who was a good friend of Jane Austen's when they were young. Although Jane Austen died in 1817 before this case came to court, it features many places and people she would have known.

The principal places concerned are the village of Ashe where the testator was rector, Ewshott House in Crondall where the plaintiffs lived and Overton where the family held lands. These are all within a few miles of Steventon where Jane Austen lived.

There are actually two cases, with slightly different parties in 1825 and 1832. The initial disagreement arises over the execution of the will of the testator, Revd John Henry George Lefroy, the plaintiffs

177

claiming that the legacies and purposes of the will are not being executed appropriately by defendants Benjamin Lefroy and James Quilter. The second case is a revival of the first to account for a change in the family's circumstances. Benjamin Lefroy, the executor, died and left his own executors in charge of the executorship of the testator's estate. In addition, one of the female Lefroy plaintiffs has got married and is therefore entitled to her inheritance, and also two Lefroy infants have died.

C 13/2193/27
Document type: Bill and two Answers.
Plaintiffs: Sophia Lefroy and others.
Defendant: Charles Edward Lefroy, Benjamin Lefroy, John Quilter, Henry Rice and wife and Christopher Edward Lefroy (abroad).
Amended by an order dated 1 November 1825: James Sheffield Brooks added as defendant.
Revived and Supplementary bill Michaelmas 1831.
JFP
Date: 1825.

C 13/2193/35
Document type: Two Answers.
Plaintiffs: Sophia Lefroy and others.
Defendant: Charles Edward Lefroy, Benjamin Lefroy, John Quilter, Henry Rice and wife and Christopher Edward Lefroy (abroad).
Amended by an order dated 1 November 1825: James Sheffield Brooks added as defendant.
Revived and Supplementary bill Michaelmas 1831.
Date: 1825.

C 13/2027/10
Document type: Examination.
Plaintiffs: Sophia Lefroy and others.

Defendant: Charles Edward Lefroy, Benjamin Lefroy, John
Quilter, Henry Rice and wife and Christopher Edward
Lefroy (abroad).
Amended by an order dated 1 November 1825: James
Sheffield Brooks added as defendant.
Revived and Supplementary bill Michaelmas 1831.
Date: 1827.

C 13/2254/1
Document type: Bill and Answer.
Plaintiffs: Sophia Lefroy and others.
Defendants: James Quilter, Jane Anna Elizabeth Lefroy,
Christopher Edward Lefroy and James Edward Austen.
Original bill Hilary 1825.
Date: 1832.

There are also over forty Orders relating to the case, Petitions and
Masters' Reports. There are so many documents with so much
information that only a taste of this can be given here, the transcript
running to 150 pages of typed text!

In summary, the testator Revd John Henry George Lefroy died,
leaving money and land in his will to various family members. It is
this will, dated 21 December 1819, just two years after the death of
the author Jane Austen, which forms the central theme of the
dispute. The case is brought by the testator's widow Sophia Lefroy,
and all their infant children apart from the eldest surviving son
Charles, who is one of the defendants, along with the executors.
What is at stake is the inheritance of the younger children and an
accusation that the executors have not managed the estate properly
and that they may not receive the full amount that is due to them
when they reach the age of 21.

The result is that not only do we find a great deal of genealogical
information, but there is also local history in the form of the lands
held by the family, and of course literary history in that this is a
family that was well known to Jane Austen. A certain amount of
social history can also be gleaned from the accounts.

THE SCHEDULES
As part of the case there are nine very detailed Schedules which are full of useful information:

The First Schedule
- Describes the freehold and copyhold estates in England and Wales of which the testator was seised at the time of his decease.
- First part: description of parts of the estate left to the testator's first son and his heir: freehold and copyhold.
- Second part: description of the testator's freehold by his will devised to be sold.

The Second Schedule
- Describes the leasehold estates of which the testator was seised at the time of his decease.

The Third Schedule
- Describes the sums of money collected and received by the defendant Benjamin Lefroy on account of the testator's personal estate since his decease.

The Fourth Schedule
- Describes the sums of money collected and received by the defendant James Quilter on the testator's personal estate since his decease and of the monies produced by sale of the leasehold estates and raised by sale of timber on the testator's estates.

The Fifth Schedule
- Outgoings of Benjamin Lefroy on account of the testator's personal estate.

The Sixth Schedule
- Payments made by James Quilter for the testator's funeral

and testamentary expenses and his debts due and the
annuity given to plaintiff Sophia Lefroy.

The Seventh Schedule

- Accounts of the rents and profits of the freehold and
copyhold estates given to the testator's first son that have
accrued between the dates of the decease of the testator and
the decease of his first son (George Lefroy) and have been
received by James Quilter.
- Second part: payments made by Quilter for this account.

The Eighth Schedule

- Accounts of the rents and profits of the freehold and
copyhold estates given to his first son accrued since the
death of George Lefroy and received by James Quilter.
- Second part: payments made by Quilter for this account.

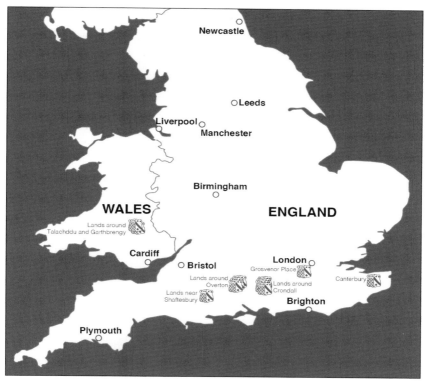

A map showing the location of lands held by Lefroy family.

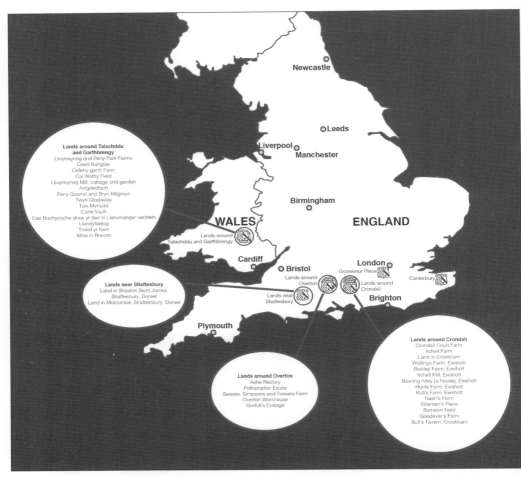

The location of lands held by the Lefroy family showing names of individual holdings.

The Ninth Schedule
• Accounts of money produced by sale of timber by defendants from the testator's estates entitled to the first son and respective issue.

GENEALOGICAL INFORMATION
There is a huge amount of genealogical information, and to summarise, the important people are:

Sophia Lefroy and Revd John Henry George Lefroy's Family

The Revd John Henry George Lefroy – testator

Sophia Lefroy – plaintiff, married to testator

George Lefroy – their eldest son, died 15 March 1824

Anne Lefroy – a plaintiff/daughter, married John McClintock the younger on 7 (or 11 as the defendants claim) August 1829

Charles Edward Lefroy – second, but eldest surviving son

Anthony Cottrell Lefroy – plaintiff/third son, aged under 21 in 1832

Frances Phoebe Lefroy – plaintiff/daughter, aged under 21 in 1832

Frederick William Lefroy – plaintiff/son, aged under 21 on 10 October 1828, probably born after 1819 as not mentioned in his father's will

Sophia Anna Lefroy – plaintiff/daughter, aged under 21 in 1832

Lucy Jemima Lefroy – plaintiff/daughter, died aged under 21 on 29 October 1827

John Henry Lefroy – plaintiff/fourth eldest son, aged under 21 in 1832

Henry Maxwell Lefroy – plaintiff/fifth eldest son, aged under 21 in 1832

Isabella Elizabeth Lefroy – plaintiff/daughter, aged under 21 in 1832

The McClintocks

John McClintock the younger – marries Anne Lefroy (of Cheltenham in Gloucestershire)

William Bunbury McClintock – John McClintock's brother (of Drumcar in the County of Louth, Ireland) a lieutenant in the Navy

Frederick William Pitt McClintock of Drumcar

John McClintock the Elder – John McClintock the younger and William Bunbury's father

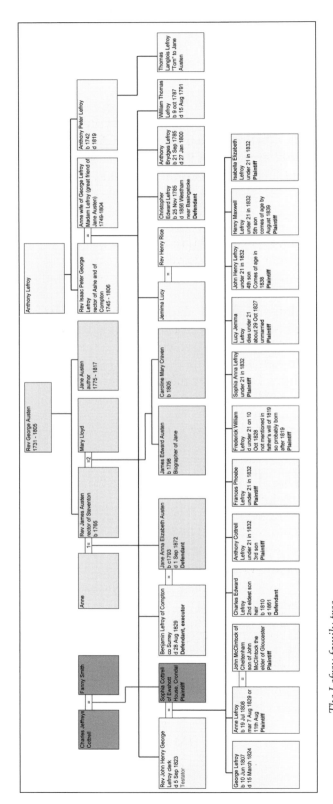

The Lefroy family tree.

The Cottrells

Charles Jeffreys Cottrell – Sophia Lefroy's father

Fanny Smith – Charles Jeffreys Cottrell's wife, this is probably Sophia's mother although it is not specified

Revd Clement Cottrell, Clerk – mentioned in the marriage indentures

The Lefroys

Benjamin Lefroy – defendant and younger brother of John Henry George Lefroy, the testator

Jemima Lucy Lefroy – sister of John Henry George Lefroy, the testator

Christopher Edward Lefroy – brother of John Henry George Lefroy, the testator, abroad for the case

Jane Anna Elizabeth Lefroy – maiden name Austen, married to Benjamin Lefroy

Captain Anthony Lefroy – mentioned in the Bill as giving the testator a note of hand

Other Important People to the Case

James Quilter – testator's friend and executor

George Glover – auctioneer and appraiser, Basingstoke

Revd Benjamin Evans – Charles Edward Lefroy's guardian who answers for him

James Edward Austen – Jane Anna Elizabeth Lefroy's brother; Benjamin Lefroy's brother-in-law

James Sheffield Brooks of John Street Bedford Row in the county of Middlesex – the man to whom Jemima Lucy Lefroy and Revd Henry Rice promise their £100 and £200 legacies from the testator

Revd Henry Rice – married to Jemima Lucy Lefroy

Charles Evans of the City of Norwich

W. Dowesdell – Master of the Court

The accounts show that payments were made for the erection of monuments in churches such as £39 for a monument in Ashe church

The interior of Crondall church.

186

for Revd John Henry George Lefroy the testator, and £20 for a tablet to be erected in Crondall church for George Lefroy, the eldest son who died in 1823.

THE WILL

This mostly concerns lands and the profits therefrom. The bequest to his eldest son is reasonably straightforward:

> all that his manor of Ewshott and all those his freehold and copyhold messuages, lands, tenements and hereditaments situate lying and being in Ewshott aforesaid and in Crondall and Crockham or elsewhere within the parish of Crondall in the said County of Southampton with their and every of their rights' to his brother Reverend Benjamin Lefroy of Compton in the County of Surrey and James Quilter of Hadley in the County of Middlesex in trust for his eldest son, and then in tail to the younger sons.

The rest of the will is very much more complicated and includes such bequests as lands for the testator's brothers, Christopher Edward Lefroy, Benjamin Lefroy and his sister Jemima Lucy, wife of the Revd Henry Rice, who are to share some of the profits with the testator's children:

- One-twelfth to Christopher Edward Lefroy and his heirs and assigns.
- One-twelfth to Benjamin Lefroy and his heirs and assigns.
- One-twelfth to Jemima Lucy Rice upon trust during her natural life to pay the rents, issues and profits into her hands for her sole and separate use, going to her heirs when she dies.
- Three-twelfth parts to go to George Lefroy (testator's oldest son) upon him reaching 23 years. If he should die under 23 then this goes to the next oldest of the testator's sons who should live to attain the said age of 23 and as such to his heirs.

- The six equal remaining twelfth parts were to be split equally between the testator's remaining children (then born and thereafter to be born – except the eldest who already has his share), their heirs and assigns. If any of these younger children die before 21, his /her part is divided equally between the survivors.
- If the number of these younger children living to 21 is reduced to four, then the equal six shares should be split equally between the eldest child and the four younger.

Perhaps most important for the case was the fact that he bequeathed his sons Charles Edward Lefroy, Anthony Cottrell Lefroy, John Henry Lefroy, Henry Maxwell Lefroy and any to be born after, at the age of 21, £1,000 each with interest from the date of his death at 5 per cent. There are many other bequests and indentures following the death of the testator mentioned in the case.

TIMELINE OF THE IMPORTANT EVENTS

21 December 1819	Testator's will published.
21 July 1823	Codicil to the will published.
5 September 1823	Testator dies.
15 March 1824	George Lefroy (the eldest son) dies, leaving Charles Edward Lefroy the eldest son and heir.
19 March 1825	First case dated (amended by order 1 November 1825).

After this date Charles Edward Lefroy (surviving second son – now eldest son) is added as a defendant.

1 August 1825	The Answer of Charles Edward Lefroy (by his guardian).
27 October 1825	The joint Answer of Revd Benjamin Lefroy and James Quilter.

3 November 1825	The joint Answer of Revd Henry Rice and Jemima Lucy his wife.
5 January 1826	The Answer of James Sheffield Brooks.
10 June 1826	Interlocutory Order: ordered that George Glover appointed as Receiver of the rents and profits of the Manors/Estates of the testator entailed on male issue and of leasehold manor/farm 'Crondall Court Farm'.
16 June 1826	Another Decree declared the will was well proved, and the trusts should be executed; Master to look into the accounts, and to look at what remains, what needs to be sold (which will then be sold with the application of the master), whether the money raised has been raised, etc.; Receiver appointed on the Order of 29 November 1825 should continue; until the sale, accounts to be passed before said Master.
1 November 1831	Bill amended by order: James Sheffield Brooks added as a defendant.
1827	Examinations.
29 October 1827	Lucy Jemima Lefroy (infant child plaintiff) dies.
12 May 1828	Master's Report: Decisions on money and accounts.
20 May 1828	Master's Report: Certified what he believed were the debts, legacies, annuitants. Certifies what should go to Sophia Lefroy and for the maintenance of her children.
23 May 1828	Plaintiffs present their Petition to the court, stating that Crondall Court Farm was sold in 1827.
5 June 1828	Plaintiff Petition asking that the reports of 20 May 1828 be realised and maintenance towards her children be paid.

20 October 1828	Frederick William Lefroy (infant child plaintiff) dies.
10 February 1829	Another Order, resulting from Petition regarding the death of a son of the testator and Sophia Lefroy, Frederick William Lefroy, and more decisions regarding money and accounts.
19 July 1829	Anne Lefroy (plaintiff and daughter) turns 21.
August 1829	Anne Lefroy marries John McClintock – reference to further settlements of indenture (June 1806; 3 September 1763).
28 August 1829	Defendant and trustee Benjamin Lefroy dies, appointing his wife Jane Anna Elizabeth Lefroy, his brother Christopher Edward Lefroy and his brother-in-law James Edward Austen his executors.
10 January 1832	Second case.

The Orders tend to refer mostly to the release of money and payment of bequests when the children reached the age of 21, or married – in the case of the girls.

LOCAL HISTORY

A large number of places are named in the documents, and anyone studying these places, or carrying out a house history, would find the references of interest. Equity court records can always throw up surprises, such as that this family, who seem so well established in Hampshire, had extensive lands in Wales and also lands in Dorset, though of course the lands at Ashe, where the testator, his brother and father had all been the rector, and at Crondall and Ewshott in Hampshire are the most numerous.

Lands in Hampshire

Ewshott House

Seaxes, Simpsons and Twiners Farms in the tithing of Ewshott

Crondall
Crondall Court Farm
Crookham
Polhampton Estate
Itchell Farm – farm house, buildings and 400 acres of land in
    Ewshott, Parish of Crondall
Wallings Farm, Ewshott, Crondall
Bickley Farm, Ewshott, Crondall
Itchell Mill, Ewshott, Crondall
Bowling Alley (a house), Ewshott, Crondall
Hunts Farm, Ewshott, Crondall
Bamskin Field, Ewshott
Bull's Farm, Crookham
Manor of Crondall
Nash's Farm
Small piece of land called Stilemans Piece in or near
    Pepperstick Lane in Crondall
Overton Workhouse
Godull's Cottage, Overton
Goodeve's Farm, Ewshott
Bull's Tavern, Crookham
Pilridding Moor
Rectory at Ashe
Ashe
Overton
Bunny's Cottage, Overton

A modern road name reflecting the Lefroy connection with Crondall.

In addition to a good amount of information on the tenants and the rents they paid, there are also details of how some of the lands are held, such as:

- Dean and Chapter of Winchester – rents for Crondall Court Farm.
- E. Broule Esq. receiver for Lord Grosvenor rent on house in Grosvenor Place.
- Marquis of Winchester for composition for great tithe for the house and land at Ewshott and coppices in hand for 1822 and 1823.
- Revd James Ogle – Vicarial tithes for house and lands in Ewshott.

Lands in Wales
Talachddu, Brecon
Mines in Brecon
Garthbrengi, Brecon
Llioyneynog and Peny Park Farms in the parish of Talachddu
Coed Bunglas, where John Jones farms
Cefeny-garth Farm in the Parish of Talachddu which includes
  a field called Cae Ycha
Bunglas Farm and Cal Wathy field in Talachddu
Llivyneynog Mill and cottage and garden, Talachddu
Dwelling house/cottage and garden called Arrgoedfach in
  Talachddu
Dwelling house, barn and garden called Peny Quarrel in
  Talachddu and a piece of land called Byrn Milgroyn
House, outhouse, garden called Twyn Glandiwlas,
  TalachdduTaix mynydd Back in Talachddu
Dwelling house, stable, barn, main house, two beast houses,
  two gardens in Carle Bach in Garthbrengy and a parcel of
  land called Cae Buchycoche draw yr dwr in the Hamlet of
  Llanvikangel vechem in Parish of Llandefeilog/Llandyfaelog

Lands in Dorset
  Shaston Saint James, Shaftesbury, Dorset
  Motcombe, Shaftesbury, Dorset

Some of the most interesting records in this case are the accounts that are provided to show how the executors have managed the estate. The Schedules, which give a huge amount of detail on the value of the estate, include names of tenants, such as:

  Several small pieces of land in the said Tithing of Ewshott and Parish of Crondall containing the several quantities and let by the said Testator in his life time to and now in the occupation of the several persons at the several yearly rents following that is to say:

Two acres let to James Stephens at per Annum	£2 0s. 0d.
1a.2r.0p let to William Mylum at per annum	£1 10s. 0d.
1a.2r.0p let to Joseph Prizeman at per annum	£1 10s. 0d.
1a.2r.0p let to John Hoare at per annum	£1 10s. 0d.
1a.2r.0p let to Daniel Bushell at per annum	£1 10s. 0d.

Other payments show the responsibility of being a landlord, such as 11s. 6d. paid to a bricklayer for repairing damage by wind to Goodull's Cottage at Overton.

SOCIAL HISTORY
After pages of details of the lands held, their rents, etc., there follow pages of accounts showing expenditure to a wide number of people. The inclusion of wine merchants and the carriage of wine bottles make for interesting reading, as do the entries relating to the education of the children. Anyone wishing to study the way of life of a reasonably well-to-do family in the early nineteenth century could spend many hours studying these accounts, which include such items as:

Dr Gabel's School – eldest son to study.

Dr Williams – board and tuition of G. Lefroy at Winchester
    School 1823 until his death.

D. Gabel, Master of Winchester School – bill for testator's
    two eldest sons.

Miss Brown, governess.

Mr Heath – carriage of wine bottles.

Henry Nicholls, wine merchant, Farnham.

Elizabeth Attwood, wine merchant, Basingstoke.

Health wine merchants, Andover.

Budden, Tailor, Basingstoke – bill for mourning for testator's
    male servants as ordered per will.

John Andrews, chandler – Crondall.

Revd Martin Smith – for materials for repairs at Court Farm.

Edward Ellis – work done at Ewshott House and Hothouse.

John Ellson, tailor – for a suit of clothes for the gamekeeper.

Richard Ware, woodman.

Messrs Lees & Co. – for iron hurdles for fence at Ewshott
    House.

Isaac Granstone – bricklayer's work at Rishman's Farm.

John Draper – powder and shot for the gamekeeper.

James White – deals sent to Ewshott House for general
    repairs.

George Lining – for noticeboard against trespassers.

Society for Promoting Christian Knowledge, Basingstoke – for
    books.

Bible Society, Basingstoke – for books.

Sarah Lyford, mantua maker, Basingstoke.

Poinchier Dancing Masters, Winchester.

J. McCallan & Co., tailors, Leicester Square.

Some entries evoke sympathy such as the payment of £1 19s. 6d.
to a hairdresser to attend the testator during his illness, and the
many charitable bequests show how the family treated those who
were not so well off.

As if this case had not already provided enough information, we next find that the large number of employees are mentioned by name, illustrating the wide social range of people that are mentioned in records of the courts of equity. These include:

John Crook, gardener, Ewshott
James Lunn, bailiff, Ewshott
Henry Liney, gardener, Ashe
Mary Ann Camis, nursery maid, Ashe
Hester Boham, housekeeper
John Haggart, the footman
Maria Cooper, the housemaid
Miss Brown, the governess
William Hockley, coachman
Susan Leach, nursery maid
Mary Kimber, kitchen maid

There are then some fairly random references which are worth a mention and again shine a light on the way of life for this type of family at this date:

• Sophia Lefroy receives money from the Sun Fire Office as compensation for damage done by the fire at Court Farm House.
• For cash paid for expenses of a witness at Winchester Spring Assizes 1825 to give evidence as to the late fire at Court House Farm.
• For cash paid W. Bymore 21 October for information against E. Pithers for injuring trees on which she was convicted.
• For cash paid Richard Ware, woodman for watching by night on Ewshott Common during the summer of 1825 to prevent depredations.

LITERARY INTEREST

There is of course no reference to the author Jane Austen in the documents, as she had died some years before the case came to court. However, there is a huge amount of background information on the people in whose social circle she moved, their names and places of course, but perhaps more interestingly, the information that emerges from the accounts relating to their way of life. These are people she knew, houses she was familiar with, perhaps farm cottages she might have visited. And of course the link with Tom Lefroy is well known. Tom does not feature in the legal case, as he was not of the immediate family, being a first cousin of the Revd John Henry George Lefroy, the testator, as their fathers were brothers. The testator's father was Revd Isaac Peter George Lefroy who was also rector of Ashe, and his wife Anne was one of Jane Austen's great friends.

The Lefroys were a provincial family, however there is some contact with London. As was seen in the section on the lands, £144 rent was paid for six years for a house in Grosvenor Place. Bills listed for London include those paid to Davison & Co., grocers in Fenchurch Street, J. Cottrell, a wax chandler in Kensington, and J. McCallan & Co., tailors in Leicester Square, another tailor in Falcon Square and W. Bradley of Tottenham Court Road for newspapers. For the ladies perhaps the bill to Eades & Westgarth, milliners of Burlington Street was the most important. Having said this, most of the bills refer to the local towns of Basingstoke, Andover and Winchester.

SUMMARY

This case was initially looked at in the hope that there would be a reference to Jane Austen; instead, a real treasure trove of information was uncovered, which serves as a final illustration of the complexity, variety and true richness of the records of the courts of equity for historians of families, houses, villages, and social status, and even literary biographers.

GLOSSARY

THE DOCUMENTS

Pleadings – Usually the Bills and Answers only and not the peripheral documents

Proceedings – Can refer to all court records, generally associated with the Court of Chancery

Bill of Complaint – The document which opens the case brought by the plaintiff

Answer – Response by defendant to the Bill of Complaint, under oath

Replication – Plaintiff's response to an Answer

Rejoinder – Defendant's response to a replication

Demurrer – Indication by the defendant that there is no case to answer

Interrogatory – List of questions set by the plaintiff or the defendant

Deposition – Answer to list of questions set by the plaintiff or the defendant

Examination – Usually the response by the defendant to specific questions to add information to his Answer

Affidavit – Statement made under oath

Petition – Request by one of the parties for an Order to be made

Order – Interim or procedural Orders

Final Order – Final decisions of the court

Decree – Final decision of the court, made absolute, not allowing any further action

Master's Report – Report by one of the Masters in response to a specific request by the judge, to investigate particular facts such as financial accounts

Exhibits – Documents used as evidence that remained with the court after the case was closed

Master's Documents – Paperwork connected to the case, held by
the Master

THE PEOPLE

Plaintiff – The person bringing the case

Orator/oratrix – Another word for plaintiff, used in the Bill of
Complaint

Complainant – Another word for plaintiff, used in the defendant's
Answer and most other records

Defendant – The person defending the case brought by the
plaintiff

Infant – A person under the age 21

Next friend – A person representing a party to the case, usually a
child but can be a woman.

Deponent – A person giving a deposition or answers to a list of
questions set by the plaintiff or defendant

Master – Officer of the court who investigated the evidence
(including Depositions, Affidavits and Exhibits), administered
the estates that were in Chancery care during the (often very
lengthy) course of a suit, and reported to the court

Counsel – Legal representative of the plaintiff or defendant

Testator – Person leaving a will which is now the subject of the
dispute

THE COURTS OF EQUITY

The following explains what the courts cover:

Chancery – The principal equity court
Exchequer – Financial matters
Requests – Poor people
Star Chamber – Violence, perjury
Palatinate of Chester – Counties of Chester and Flint
Palatinate of Durham – County of Durham

Palatinate of Lancaster – County of Lancaster
Duchy of Lancaster – Lands all over the country held by the Duchy
of Lancaster

THE COMMON LAW COURTS
(These are not the subject of this book)
Court of the King's Bench
Court of Common Pleas

THE INDEXES
Index – Fully alphabetical list
Calendar – Usually alphabetical by first letter of principal surname
then chronological
List – Usually in order of document reference
Catalogue – In order of document reference
Discovery – The online catalogue for The National Archives

SELECT BIBLIOGRAPHY

Adams, John and Ralston, Robert. *The doctrine of equity: a commentary on the law as administered by the Court of chancery*, T. & J.W. Johnson, 1855

Atkyns, Sir Robert. *Enquiry into the Jurisdiction of the Chancery in causes of Equity*, 1695

Avery, M.E. 'An Evaluation of the Effectiveness of the Court of Chancery under the Lancastrian Kings', *Law Quarterly Review*, 86 (1970), 84–97

Avery, M.E. 'The History of the Equitable Jurisdiction of Chancery before 1460', *Bulletin of the Institute of Historical Research*, 42 (1969), 129–44

Baker, J.H. *An Introduction to English Legal History*, Butterworths, 2002

Baker, J.H. *The Common Lawyer and the Chancery 1616*, repr. in his *The Legal Profession and the Common Law Historical Essays* (originally published in *The Irish Jurist*, 4, 1969, pp. 368–92), Hambledon Press, 1986, pp. 205–29

Ball, R.M. 'Tobias Eden, Change and Conflict in the Exchequer Office, 1672–1698', *Journal of Legal History*, 11 (1990)

Barnes, Thomas Garden. 'Star Chamber Mythology', *The American Journal of Legal History*, Vol. 5, No. 1, 1961, 1–11, www.jstor.org/stable/844462

Bayne, C.G. and Dunham, W.H. (eds). *Select cases in the council of Henry VII*, Selden Society, 1958

Beresford, Maurice. 'The Decree Rolls of Chancery as a source for economic history 1547–c1700', *Economic History Review*, 2nd series, 32 (1979), 1–10

Bradford, Gladys. *Proceedings in the Court of the Star Chamber in the Reigns of Henry VII and Henry VIII*, Somerset Record Society, Vol. 27, 1911

Brooks, Christopher W. 'Interpersonal conflict and social tension: civil litigation in England 1640–1830', in A.L. Beier, David Cannadine and James M. Rosenheim (eds), *The First Modern Society*, Cambridge University Press, 1989, pp. 357–99

Brown, Ronald Stewart (ed.). *Lancashire and Cheshire cases in the Court of Star Chamber. Part I*, Vol. 71 of Record Society of Lancashire and Cheshire, printed for the Record Society, 1916

Bryson, W.H. 'The Equity Side of the Exchequer Its Jurisdiction, Administration, Procedures and Records', PhD, University of Cambridge, 1972

Carne, William Lindsay. *A Sketch of the History of the High Court of Chancery from the Chancellorship of Wolsey to That of Lord Nottingham, Virginia Law Register (Virginia Law Review)*, New Series, Vol. 13, No. 10 (1928)

Carne, William Lindsay. *A Sketch of the History of the High Court of Chancery from Its Origin to the Chancellorship of Wolsey, Virginia Law Register (Virginia Law Review)*, New Series, Vol. 13, No. 7 (1927)

Cheney, C.R. (ed.). *A Handbook of Dates for Students of British History*, new edn rev. by Michael Jones (Royal Historical Society Guides and Handbooks No. 4), Cambridge University Press, 2000

Churches, Christine. '"The most unconvincing testimony"; the genesis and historical usefulness of the country deposition in Chancery', *Seventeenth Century*, XI (1996), 209–27

Coldham, P.W. 'Genealogical Resources in Chancery Records – 2; Documents of Masters in Chancery', *Genealogical Magazine*, 19 (1977–9), 349–7

Derbyshire, Mike. *Introductory Guide to the Records of the Palatinate of Lancaster*, Rowton Books, 2016

Dwelly, E. (ed.), prepared by Adrian J. Webb. *Exchequer Depositions by Commission for Somerset 1565–1610*, privately published, 1992

D[wight], T.W. *The Jurisdiction of the Court of Chancery to Enforce Charitable Uses, American Law Register (University of Pennsylvania Law Review)*, 10 (3) (January 1862)

D[wight], T.W. *The Jurisdiction of the Court of Chancery to Enforce*

Charitable Uses (Continued), *American Law Register* (*University of Pennsylvania Law Review*), 10, (7), New Series Vol. 1 (May 1862)

Edwards, I. *A Catalogue of Star Chamber Proceedings Relating to Wales*, Cardiff University Press Board, 1929

Elton, G.R. *Star Chamber Stories*, Methuen, 1958

Fishwick, Caroline. *A Calendar of Lancashire and Cheshire Exchequer Depositions by Commission 1558–1802*, 1885

Gardiner, Samuel Rawson. *Reports of cases in the Courts of Star Chamber and High Commission*, Camden Society, 1886

Gerhold, Dorian. *Courts of Equity: A guide to chancery and other legal records for local and family historians*, Pinhorn Handbooks, 1994

Goulden, R.G. *Some Chancery Lawsuits: An Analytic List (of eighteenth century printers cases in C11)*, privately published, 1982/3

Guy, J.A. *The Cardinal's Court: the impact of Thomas Wolsey in Star Chamber*, Harvester, 1977

Guy, J.A. 'The early-Tudor Star Chamber', in D. Jenkins (ed.), *Legal History Studies*, University of Wales Press, 1975

Hanworth, Lord. 'Some Notes on the Office of Master of the Rolls', *Cambridge Law Journal* (Cambridge University Press), Vol. 5, Issue 3, November 1935, 313–31

Haskett, Timothy. 'The medieval English court of Chancery', *Law and History Review*, 14 (1996), 245–313

Haskett, Timothy. 'The Presentation of Cases in medieval Chancery Bills', in W.M. Gordon and T.D Fergus (eds), *Legal History in the Making, Proceedings of the Ninth British Legal History Conference, Glasgow, 1989*, Hambledon Press, 1991, pp. 11–28

Henderson, Edith G. 'Legal Rights to Land in the early Chancery', *American Journal of Legal History*, 26 (1982), 97–122

Horwitz, Henry. *Exchequer Equity Records and Proceedings 1649–1841*, PRO Publications, 2001

Horwitz, Henry. *A Guide to Chancery Equity Records and Proceedings 1600–1800*, PRO Publications, 1998

Horwitz, Henry. 'Continuity or Change in the Court of Chancery in the Seventeenth and Eighteenth Centuries?', *Journal of British*

Studies (University of Chicago Press) (1996), Vol. 35, No. 1 (January 1996), 24–57

Horwitz, H. and Cooke, J. *Samples of Exchequer Equity Pleadings and Suits 1685–6, 1734–5, 1784–5, and 1818–9*, List and Index Society, Vol. 278 (2000)

Horwitz, H. and Moreton, C. *Samples of Chancery Pleadings and Suits: 1628, 1685, 1735 and 1785*, List and Index Society, Vol. 257 (1995)

Hoyle, Richard W. and Summerson, Henry R.T. *A handlist of Star Chamber pleadings before 1558 for Northern England*, The National Archives, 2003

Hudson, Alastair. *Equity and Trusts* (6th edn), Routledge-Cavendish, 2009

Jacques, E.T. *Charles Dickens in Chancery*, Longham, 1914

Jones, William J. 'Conflict or Collaboration? Chancery Attitudes in the reign of Elizabeth I', *American Journal of Legal History*, 5 (1961), 12–54

Kerly, Duncan. *An historical sketch of the equitable jurisdiction of the Court of Chancery*, Cambridge University Press, 1890

Knafla, Louis A. (ed.). *Kent at Law*, Star Chamber List and Index Society Special Series No. 51, 2012

Knafla, Louis A. (ed.). *Kent at Law*, Courts of Equity: Chancery List and Index Society Special Series No. 52, 2013

Knafla, Louis A. (ed.). *Kent at Law*, Courts of Equity: Requests List and Index Society Special Series No. 53, 2014

Lawton, Guy. 'Using Bernau's notebooks', 3 parts in *Family Tree Magazine*, X 2-4 (12/1993–2/1994), 44, 21 and 15

Leadam, I.S. (ed.). *Select cases before the King's Council in the Star Chamber, commonly called the Court of Star Chamber, AD 1477–[1544]*, Selden Society, 1903

Leadam, I.S. *Select cases in the Court of Requests*, Vol. XII, Selden Society, 1898

Lobban, Michael. 'Preparing for Fusion: Reforming the Nineteenth-Century Court of Chancery, Part I', *Law and History Review* (University of Illinois Press) 22 (2) (Spring 2004), 389–427

Mann, J.H. *Chancery Depositions taken by Commission. A complete list of all such depositions for the county of Devonshire as are filed among the Chancery Proceedings 1714–1758 at the Public Record Office London*, Public Record Office, 1950

McDermott, Peter M. 'Jurisdiction of the Court of Chancery to award damages', *Law Quarterly Review* (Sweet and Maxwell), 108 (1992)

McKendrick, Ewan. *Contract Law* (7th edn), Palgrave Macmillan, 2007

Marsh, Alfred Henry. *History of the Court of Chancery and of the rise and development of the doctrines of equity*, Carswell & Co., 1890

Milhous, J. and Hume, R. 'Eighteenth century Equity lawsuits in the Court of the Exchequer as a source for historical research', *Historical Research* 70 (1997), 231–46

Monro, C. *Acta Cancellariae: or Selections from the Records of the Court of Chancery Remaining in the Office of Reports and Entries*, 1847

Moore, S.T. *Family Feuds, An Introduction to Chancery Proceedings*, Federation of Family History Societies, 2002

Parkes, Joseph. *A history of the Court of chancery; with practical remarks on the recent commission, report, and evidence, and on the means of improving the administration of justice in the English courts of equity*, Longman, 1828

Peel, Edwin. *The Law of Contract* (12th edn), Sweet and Maxwell, 2007

Plucknet, Theodore. *A Concise History of the Common Law*, Liberty Fund, 2010

Ritchie, John (ed.). *Reports of Cases decided by Francis Bacon in the High Court of Chancery*, Sweet and Maxwell, 1932

Sanders, G.W. *The Orders of the High Court of Chancery*, 1845

Snell, F.S. (ed.). 'A calendar of Chancery Depositions before 1714', *The British Archivist*, I (1913–20), supplement 2

Stretton, Tim. 'Women and Litigation in the Elizabethan Court of Requests', PhD, University of Cambridge, 1993

Trowles, T. 'Eighteenth Century Exchequer Records as a

Genealogical Source', *Genealogists Magazine*, 25 (1995), 93–8

Tucker, P. 'The Early History of the Court of Chancery: A Comparative Study', *English Historical Review* (Oxford University Press), 115 (463) (2000), 791–811

Yale, D.E.C. (ed.). *Lord Nottingham's 'Manual of Chancery Practice' and 'Prolegomena of Chancery and Equity'*, Cambridge University Press, 1965

NOTES

Preface
1. TNA reference STAC 2/8.

Chapter 1
1. J.H. Baker, *An Introduction to English Legal History*, Butterworths, 2002.
2. Ibid.
3. *Reports of Cases Taken and Adjudged in the Court of Chancery* (3rd edn, 1736) as quoted in Louis A. Knafla (ed.), *Kent at Law*, List and Index Society Special Series No. 51, 2012 and *Kent at Law*, Courts of Equity: Chancery List and Index Society Special Series No. 52, 2013.
4. Sir Robert Atkyns, *Enquiry into the Jurisdiction of the Chancery in Causes of Equity*, 1695.
5. W. Lambarde, *Archeion*, 1635, p. 116.
6. 5 Elizabeth, cap.9c.
7. Theodore Plucknet, *A Concise History of the Common Law*, Liberty Fund, 2010.
8. Henry Horwitz, *A Guide to Chancery Equity Records and Proceedings, 1600–1800*, PRO Publications, 1998.
9. Knafla (ed.), *Kent at Law*, List and Index Society Special Series No. 51 and *Kent at Law*, Courts of Equity: Chancery List and Index Society Special Series No. 52.
10. C.R. Cheney (ed.), *A Handbook of Dates for Students of British History*, new edn rev. by Michael Jones (Royal Historical Society Guides and Handbooks No. 4), Cambridge University Press, 2000.
11. *The Compleat Clerk*, published 1677.
12. Horwitz, *A Guide to Chancery Equity Records* and Henry Horwitz, *Exchequer Equity Records and Proceedings 1649–1841*, PRO Publications, 2001.

13. Knafla (ed.), *Kent at Law*, Courts of Equity: Chancery List and Index Society Special Series No. 52.
14. See Horwitz, *Exchequer Equity Records*.

Chapter 2
1. TNA reference C 11/1987/27.
2. TNA reference C 7/1133/39.
3. TNA reference C 13/1329/11.
4. TNA reference C 11/1674/19.
5. TNA reference C 6/370/6.
6. TNA reference C 13/92/13.
7. TNA reference C 5/432/52.
8. TNA reference C 6/145/154.
9. TNA reference C 6/357/16.
10. TNA reference C 6/364/1.
11. TNA reference C 6/374/68.
12. TNA reference C 6/58/117.
13. TNA reference C 11/468/31.
14. TNA reference E 134/5Geo2/Mich27.
15. TNA reference C 11/789/15.
16. TNA reference C 110/35.
17. TNA reference C 13/27/28.
18. TNA reference C 14/1064/V12.
19. TNA reference C 22/976/9.
20. TNA reference C 3/8/113.

Chapter 3
1. TNA reference C 11/468/31.
2. TNA reference C 13/721/4.
3. TNA reference DL 1/444.
4. TNA reference PL 6/34/112.
5. TNA reference C 11/2770/12.
6. TNA reference DL 4/146/1751/1.
7. TNA reference PL 10/122.
8. TNA reference C 33/959, f. 605.
9. TNA reference C 38/262.
10. TNA reference C 38/262.

11. TNA reference C 38/5.
12. TNA reference C 111/99.
13. TNA reference C 110/80.
14. TNA reference C 109/339.
15. TNA reference C 110/173.
16. TNA reference C 103/18.
17. TNA reference C 108/174.
18. TNA reference C112/163.
19. TNA reference C 41/13.
20. TNA reference C 41/42.
21. TNA reference C 36/14.
22. TNA reference C 13/348/5.

Chapter 5
1. TNA reference C 11/376/102.
2. TNA reference C 13/1766/27.
3. TNA reference C 13/721/4.
4. TNA reference C 7/133/39.
5. TNA reference C 7_133_39.
6. TNA reference C 6/375/19.
7. TNA reference C 6/408/52.
8. TNA reference C 6/345/70.
9. TNA reference C 5/59/44.
10. TNA reference C 11/666/16.
11. TNA reference STAC 3/3/80.
12. TNA reference STAC 8/109/18.

INDEX